Just Because
I'M MIXED
DOESN'T MEAN
I'M CONFUSED

Empowering Within and
Discovering Your Hairitage

By Svenya Nimmons

To the Chavez family 4.15.11

♡,

Especially Kathleen + Lizette

Svenya

ISBN-13:
978-1453880869

ISBN-10:
1453880860

For bulk or wholesale orders, please contact the author at
www.SwirlPower.com

For my Family and Godchildren (especially Mekailyn, Mariah and Maurice)

God's promises really do have a purpose. The way it plays out is the amazing part.

Thanks for being a part of mine.

TABLE OF CONTENTS

Acknowledgements

The first time I finished writing this book I felt as if a weight had been lifted off my shoulders. Everything that I had ever wanted to say to the next generation and my peers had finally been laid down on paper. I could finally breathe again. As time went by I realized that it was missing something. It was missing me. I had only written about the things that I wanted to expose and I had kept some of those memories to myself for the sake of keeping my life somewhat personal. I didn't want to be labeled anymore names as I had already endured over the years nor did I want to be looked as another stereotypical, misguided mixed girl. But then it hit me. If I was going to motivate others about living a life without confusion, I needed to uncover my whole self. If not, why else was I writing? I had to dig deeper. So I did, and this is what I dug up.

This book would not have been possible without those that have supported me along the way. Every conversation brought more fire and confirmation that I was on the right path to follow through with living out part of my given purpose in life. The beginning was very discouraging as I struggled to find a literary agent interested in my topic. Ironically, no one was interested in a book about people that no one was interested in. I didn't understand why no one cared about the problems of biracial people, yet everyone knows at least one biracial person. As frustrating as it was to hear the countless rejections, I moved forward. If no one was willing to take on the task, I just had to do it myself. Since then, I've been blessed with the help and support of others that no agent could have ever given me. I never would have imagined in a million years that I'd be writing a book. It was never something that I had considered. I never even thought I had a voice. But I do. And now I can't shut up.

I owe the biggest thanks to George Hughes who took the time to see my vision and put so much of his support in it that I often forgot that I still had a lot of work to do. To Anna Fuson and Matthew Jordan Smith, you both believed in me without hesitation and it has truly been an honor to have your support.. Because of you, I feel like I have my voice back. You both make me look good in your own way and I love you for it! To Alisa Barnes, Vince McBee, Nick Cooper, Tony Reese, Fred Johnson, James Muhammad and Marva Farris, thank you for your professional expertise throughout the entire process. I've truly had the best of everything.

Lastly, I'd like to thank my loving family and friends. Just having you in my life is a blessing of laughs, love and lessons that will never leave my heart. To my mom and dad, you've given me nothing but the best and I wouldn't change a thing. I love you both more than you can imagine and I'm the luckiest daughter in the world. To my aunts, uncle, sister and godmother, thank you for believing in me without even knowing what this whole "book thing" was all about. Thank you Grandma Barb and the Pratt family for your constant love. I'm so proud to call you my family. To my god children; Mekailyn,

Brandi, Ymani, Justin, Kenny, and Jeremy, there is nothing in life that you can't have but it takes more than a desire. It takes focus and discipline. As soon as you start to lose one, you'll lose the other and the more you concentrate on one, you'll gain the other. Whichever way you decide to go is totally up to you.

I dedicate my work and effort in loving memory of Terri Nimmons, my grandparents, and my dear friend Kellie.

Give Me the "Spot" Light

"Daddy, whatcha' doin?" I asked. It had been a long time since I had seen my dad downstairs in the den, listening to his records. But as long as I could remember, I had never seen him stacking them up and placing them carefully in boxes as if they were newborn babies being laid to rest in their crib.

"I'm just putting up my records so you won't step on them and break them," he answered me without looking up. It sounded like it made sense. I tended to break things when I got excited.

But that day there was something different. Daddy didn't have that same sparkle in his eyes when I was in his presence. He didn't even acknowledge me with his eyes when I pranced down the hallway. Something was wrong and it was up to me to make him feel better.

Daddy laid down on the floor and placed the headphones on his ears. It looked like somebody needed a little sunshine. Thank goodness I was available.

This time my presence wasn't enough to make the clouds go away. Still not satisfied with the lack of attention I was receiving, I sat down beside him as he took the earphones off his head and unplugged them from the stereo. The room was filled with the sounds of Al Green. I got closer to my daddy and he rubbed my hands as Al sang of his heartbreak. Must have been those hot grits his wife threw at him to make a man sound so hurt that it stings. That was the last day I remembered my dad calling our house his home.

I never really understood the whole concept of divorce growing up. It wasn't until later that I realized that Daddy wasn't at the house after work because he wasn't married to Momma anymore. I'm grateful that I didn't go through the nightmare of divorce that I read about in books. My dad had a really cool girlfriend that braided my hair when my brother and I visited Daddy every other weekend. While at home, my god mother BJ and her two sons had moved in with us. Not only did I live with my most favorite person in the world, but now I had two more brothers to show me the latest wrestling moves. Everywhere I went life was good; even on Sundays. We would go to church where I'd sit on the pew with my brother, my dad, his girlfriend, her two sons, her sister Wanda, and Momma.

Momma was the only white lady in the whole congregation, but she was always cooler than a fan. I don't know how she conjured up enough guts to go to the same church with her ex-husband and his new girlfriend. It would have taken Jesus and all his disciples to carry *me* out of there!

The only time I remember seeing my mother show any emotion about being alone was the day my brother Damon and I were fighting upstairs. A few months after Daddy moved out, the rain had kept my brother and I in the house. Unfortunately for him, I was the kid sister to the third degree and annoying him was my obligation. He would lock me out of his room and I would write on a piece of paper, "You stink. P. U." That particular day, I finally got on his last nerve and he fought back. As easy going as he was, this particular day I had pushed his last button and he snapped. With his tongue out the side of his mouth, he ran to me and it startled me. I didn't know he had it in him! As I yelled downstairs to my mom sitting on the couch, my brother Damon yelled louder before I could even get a lie out of my mouth.

"Stop it right now!" Momma yelled at us. "Stop!" tears ran down her face.

"Momma, what's wrong?" we both asked.

"My dad died. Now stop it!" We both rushed to her and hugged her as she wailed and cried. I should have drawn Damon a pretty picture instead.

As she wiped her eyes, I felt her hurt throughout my body. My daddy and her daddy were both gone. I don't know if I said anything, but it didn't matter because Momma gathered enough of her own strength and pulled herself together.

I later found out that my grandfather had passed away two weeks before my mother was notified. A copy of the obituary was sent to the house without a note, without condolences, without anything written in the three empty pages attached to the obituary. Johanna Niemann was listed as a survivor. My mother's name is Johanna Nimmons. Ironically, Niemann is similar to term "no one" in German. After my mother left her town in Germany to move to the United States with the love of her life, a black Army man, that's what most of the family regarded her as, no one. At that time, any German woman who associated with a black man was regarded as a call girl, a prostitute. This included my mother, a biology apprentice and manager of a pharmacy.

Mom's spunky and optimistic attitude never showed any pain outside of that one dark day. I'll probably never know exactly how she stood so strong without breaking her game face. Some people are just built like that I guess.

Growing up school came pretty easy for me as far as the school work was concerned. I simply did what I was told to do and I made good grades. Not only was my mother a German woman with very strict discipline, but she was a teacher too. I was too afraid to treat my teachers with any less respect than I treated my mom. Plus, I was convinced that teachers had their own secret society. Since my daddy was also an academic achiever, he didn't expect anything less than great either. Even daddy's mother was a teacher so I had to be sure that I was very respectful at all times. Besides, knowing my grandma Ruby Nimmons, she was probably the secret society president!

My grades were never as good as my older brother Damon's, but because he had already set the tone, I made a good enough impression on the teachers without much effort. There was however one situation that my brother couldn't do anything about. There were girls at my school that wanted to fight me for any reason they could think of. This became an ongoing occurrence in the girl's bathroom and while walking home from school. On some days I got into so many fights in the girl's bathrooms that I'd walk in, fight my battle, and walk out without saying a word. When there *was* dialog, it was pretty brief and straight to the point.

"You think you're so smart."

Not really, just smarter than you.

"You think you're so cute because you have long hair."

Well…yeah. But if you knew the hours it took to wash, I think you'd choose to be as bald headed as you are now.

The girls in my class were my friends when we first met, but once my mother showed up at the Christmas program, somehow my percentage of blackness went down. I was then seen as much of a target as the three white students that made up our entire white population in the elementary school. Surely middle school would be better than this.

The Day I Realized I Was Different

I remember the day I found out why people stared at me the way they did and it wasn't because I was cute as my vanity had lead me to believe. When I was eight years old, my mother enrolled me into modern dance classes at the Community School of the Arts. The school was located in an old church in downtown Charlotte, North Carolina. I looked forward to Tuesday and Thursday classes each week and practiced at home every chance I got. My self-made weekly rehearsals consisted of a session of high kicks and leaps, an episode of *Fame*, followed by my imitations of Debbie Allen and LeRoy from that episode.

When it was time to go to class, I would carry my bag over my shoulder with my head up and shoulders back. I wanted to wear a cut off shirt like Leroy, but Momma quickly destroyed that dream so I settled for a skirt over my tights and leotard. I'd stride on into the old dance studio like I was coming to work! Debbie *owned* that dance studio every time she walked in the door and so it was only appropriate that I did the same. I always envisioned my performances with a spotlight on me and only me. The other dancers were just for scenery.

Dancing came natural to me, not necessarily because I was all that graceful, but because I was just good at mimicking my instructor. From my body alignment to my facial expressions, I studied my teacher's every move. The more I began to advance in my skills, the more confident I became to actually look at myself in the mirror. Dancing no longer seemed like awkward movements. My mind learned to relax and let my body do all the work. I finally found something that I loved that didn't involve following in my big brother's footsteps.

One winter afternoon, I hurried into class and sat anxiously on the cold polished wooden floor waiting for class to begin. I had a great "rehearsal" the night before and I

was more than eager to show off my new lavender leotard. My dance teacher instructed us to sit on the floor in the front of the class. As she reviewed the history of the maypole dance, Molly sat next to me.

When Molly talked, she seemed to talk through her nose like the librarian at my school. I smiled at Molly as if to say hello. In response she whispered to me, "You're the only black girl in the class." My heart dropped and stopped beating at the same time. I even turned towards the mirror to look at myself. Well, she was right!

Up until that moment, I actually *enjoyed* being the only brown girl in the class. I was able to spot myself out in the mirror a lot easier. But now this girl had irritated me rather than embarrassed me as she may have intended. Did this girl not see how great I was during the kick and leap lessons? I mean, hello! Honey I was fierce! She must not have cable because anyone that saw Debbie Allen on *Fame* wouldn't dare make such a stupid remark. I thought that being brown was part of the reason why I danced so well.

She said it as if I was somehow unworthy of ever being the best in the class or maybe that I should have been grateful that I was there. For the first time in my life, I was speechless. What should I say to put her in her place? Growing up in a house full of boys, I always had a comeback statement, but not this time.

The only thing I could think to do was to look at myself in the mirror again and turn my head, hoping no one else heard her.

They did.

I was disappointed, disappointed in myself. Not only because this girl clearly couldn't see my worth, but because I didn't have the courage to defend myself.

Have I Always Been This Ugly?

By age 11, my body had morphed into a shell of unfamiliarity and my need to be seen became a thing of the past. My appetite had picked up, a set of new pimples grew on my face every morning and I still had no idea why my hair seemed to swell up *and* out every day. I became so shy and self conscience that I recognized everyone in my class by their shoes. Had I been ugly this whole time? No wonder the girls didn't like me. Ugly folks never make friends easily.

I was too shy to ask my mother if I could start wearing bras. Instead I started wearing some hand me down bras from my god sister. They were too big, but at least my shirts didn't irritate my sensitive breasts anymore. When I got my first period, I had no idea what was going on. All of those *Are You There God, It's Me Margaret* books went right over my head when they talked about that stuff. I never really paid attention until I found out that I would have to start wearing those diaper-like things for a week. I wasn't too happy about that. How could I play basketball and wrestle with the fellas if I had those kinds of issues going on? I was so naïve at the time about what was really happening that I thought I was simply bleeding from the fall off of my brother's bike the day before. I had already managed to have scars from climbing trees and jumping fences already, what was the issue about having another bleeding scab?

I spent the summer before middle school, in Germany with a friend whose father was stationed in Stuttgart. I also got a chance to meet my mother's half sister, whom she had never met. It was my first time back in Germany without my mother and I felt very independent. That summer I traveled all throughout Europe and my friend and I would play *How Many Black People Will We See Today?* We never got past thirteen. That day I was so happy to see them I could have personally greeted each African on that tour bus myself!

In Italy, people would stare at us as we walked by and kids would sometimes follow us down the street while old ladies walked out on their porches as the parade walked by. When I was in a playful mood we'd teach the kids bad words in English, but

14

when they began to annoy me with their stares, I would stick my tongue out at them. As mean as I sometimes was to them, they still wanted to be my friends although I think they only adored me because they thought I was made of chocolate. I liked the attention that my brown skin brought me. It was just enough to gain back some of my black percentage points I had lost during the school year. I felt whole again. So much so, that on my next visit to Germany, I saw a Neo Nazi skinhead on the street staring me down and ready for war. These guys were known to jump Americans-especially black Americans, on the street and leave them for dead. So what did I do? I winked my eye at him as I rode away. Confidence will make you do things on the fly that you never imagine doing.

That summer was also my first time seeing another biracial person like myself. I don't remember what she looked like or even where I saw her exactly. I just remember going to bed that night and thinking that maybe Germany was where I was suppose to live because that's where us black/white girls live. Growing up, I had never heard the term "mixed" or "biracial". At that time, kids like me didn't get a real title. I just responded with, "my momma is white" if anyone asked me. Where I lived, interracial dating was taboo and not really recognized to some people as a true family. People considered it more like two people being rebellious in the name of love and as a result, they had these light brown looking babies.

Once I got to middle school, it didn't seem as much of a nightmare as I thought it would be. I was back in a school where my brother had made a path for me-again. Because of my high test scores, I managed to be placed in the advanced courses in the core subjects. Now I knew how those white kids felt at my old school. I was one of the three black people in my classes.

Although the entire school was somewhat diverse, it was the first time I had been around so many white kids my age. It was then that I realized that all white people didn't look alike and white girls had names other than Jennifer and Molly. Throughout each day, I was either on the school bus full of black kids that loved to crack jokes on each other or I was in the classroom listening to white kids in their boat shoes telling corny jokes that I wouldn't dare repeat while on the bus ride back home.

Finding My Way

Since my return back to the States, I still had not seen another biracial girl like me. My dose of sisterhood came from my girlfriends that I shared my advanced classes with. Jessica, her cousin Maria, and Kellie were funny and smart and I could be myself around them. Kellie even had a mole on her upper lip like me and long hair like me. She may not have been mixed, but she was close enough.

Unfortunately my new sisterhood of friends didn't help my grades as they began to drop. The pressure was on and I had to work a lot harder to keep up my reputation. I loved to read, but now reading books became a difficult task because it took me a couple of times to grasp the concept of what I was reading. My projects were turned in to the best of my ability although every time I got to class, the other kids seemed to have a much more polished presentation. They had word processors and computers at home to type their assignments while I just had to make sure that I used my best handwriting. Once Daddy bought us a computer, the other kids were on to cool graphics and scanners to scan photos. I had gone from being the smartest with very few friends, to being average but having enough friends to keep a busy social life. I had decided that I could live with that. Within my family, my parents got along quite well and my new stepmom, Terri or "Momma T" (the hair braiding lady from church) treated me like I was one of her own children. My stepbrothers were never called "stepbrothers," just my brothers. Momma T was so fun to be around and I enjoyed being around her. She always made sure I didn't leave the house with my hair looking the mess I had arrived with. Her hands were the only hands that my thick, unruly hair would bow down to. She made me feel pretty-just like I did before I turned ugly.

Daddy never missed an important event and I looked forward to my weekends at his house, mostly because we were able to watch *In Living Color* on Friday nights. Momma didn't let us watch shows like *Good Times* and *The Jefferson's* where they called white people derogatory names like "honky" or "cracker." Although *In Living Color* didn't use racial slurs, it was often so ridiculously funny that we thought Momma would take it away too, just because it made us laugh until we cried.

Although my body was still going through changes, I learned to get my information on what it all meant through teen magazines and books at the library. I was too shy to ask, but too smart to just sit and wonder. By the 8th grade I was introduced to the Almighty Relaxer. Kellie's mom recommended my mom to the miracle worker called a beautician.

High school was so much fun that I don't remember doing much homework although I must have been pretty good at it because I graduated with honors. Once I figured out what to do with my hair, my confidence in the classroom and amongst my peers gained momentum.

I also met my first biracial friend in high school, Melissa. She was really smart and had gone to middle school with one of my brothers so we had an instant bond during the first day of school in homeroom. After fifteen years, I finally had a friend that looked like me and understood me. I wasn't odd anymore.

When it was time to decide what college I would go to, I simply looked at the schools that had a major in advertising and applied. My favorite classes were in Marketing and I had been chosen to work on some advertising projects by my teachers. It seemed like something that was exciting and didn't involve too much math so I was sold! I chose The University of South Carolina for their College of Journalism and Mass Communications program concentrating in advertising. It was a good thing I got accepted, because it was the only school I had applied to. I didn't have a lot of money to use for the application fee so I just hoped for the best. I was so independent that I never even told my parents what school I applied to until I was accepted.

At that point, I was living at my dad and Momma T's house and was working two part-time jobs after dance rehearsal at school and on the weekends. I was given my first car; my brother's old grey *Chevrolet* so that I could get around without having to be picked up by my brother who made it quite clear that I was wrecking his social life.

A Different World: College Life

I found work by the second day of arriving on my college campus at the Office of Disabilities as a receptionist. In our department, we assisted students with physical and learning disabilities. In terms of my school work, the first semester of college left me frustrated with myself and I began to think I just wasn't smart enough. Studying in a freshman dorm was as productive as the spades tournaments in the lobby. As much as I enjoyed my classes, I couldn't focus enough to stay ahead of the class as I had done back home. Even though my job had afforded me plenty of resources, during the five years that I worked there it never occurred to me that I should be tested for a learning disability. To battle my study issues (and undetected case of ADD), I focused on being very organized and secluded in order to concentrate. I would insist on sitting up front in class to stay alert and attentive. It wasn't until ten years after graduating from college that I later found out that I actually had a learning disability

Life Happens

Between working school, two jobs, *and* dancing on the dance team (That's right Molly, and you better believe I owned the "spot" light then, too!), I somehow made it out of college with decent grades and a promising future-although I wasn't quite sure what it was yet. I moved back to my hometown of Charlotte and took a job at the local newspaper company where my brother also worked and where he once again had set up a positive reputation that I could follow. I got engaged to my college sweetheart and a few months before our wedding date, I was told that it just wasn't going to work out.

Although I had already suffered from heartbreak and disappointment in the past, this was my first known deep depression period. I had failed in my six year relationship, was betrayed by my best friend and even lost my dog in the process. I hated my job and everything about my life that I treasured was gone. Two weeks later I was unemployed and back living at my mother's house.

My first break away from it all was an opportunity to tour the US as a tour manager. It was then that I began to see that I had been living in a small world that I had built in my own mind. I enjoyed being a face that no one knew. Some towns didn't see brown girls that looked like me very often and it was like being in Europe all over again. As the different touring contracts began to pick up over the years I got used to the stares that most times were out of admiration, but some were out of racist beliefs. I learned when to turn on the charm and when to show that I wasn't a force to be reckoned with.

Just when I began to get control, my Momma T died after her fourth battle with cancer and the depression began again. I couldn't sleep at night, I couldn't concentrate on work and my mind was always in three different places at the same time. I just couldn't shake the depression. I felt like I was a disappointment to myself and even my attempts to make things better were failures. To deal with my grief, I tried to stay busy, but I only ended up with more frustration amongst a busy schedule. How did my life come to be so ordinary after all that I had experienced? Was this it for me and if so, when could I just go ahead and die? This certainly wasn't the exciting life I had dreamed of.

I decided to get back on the road this time working for a staffing company, but after four years of traveling I was laid off during the recession. Although the layoff had completely thrown me off, I wasn't all that upset about losing my job. I had the most conniving boss that could never make a decision on her own, yet got credit for everyone else's hard work. I was over being in airports every other week and dealing with white men in manufacturing settings. These men thought that because I was a young woman, I was there to play a passive role. As a young *black* woman, when I commanded their respect they assumed that I was acting like a "typical black woman." They looked surprised when I didn't snap my fingers in a circle when I spoke and somehow they felt the need to add "girlfriend" and "girl" to the end of their sentences when talking to me. I was irritated by their ignorance and my employer's negligence to have my back when I defended myself.

Besides all of the work stress, I had personal issues that made the stress even harder to deal with. I had been going non-stop for years totally ignorant to the fact that I was now in the pre-stages of diabetes and I had gained weight from eating out every day. Although my older brother had been diagnosed with insipidus diabetes already, it never occurred to me that I too, could get hit with the disease. I had been physically active all my life and even on the road, I found creative opportunities to work out regularly. Just like the learning disability, I fought through the frustration with myself totally clueless to what was going on inside of my own body. I blamed myself for not having the energy and drive to make things better.

My friend Kellie sent a text to me one day inviting me to her house for a house warming party in celebration of her 30th birthday. As I saw the text from my bedside, I desperately wanted to stop by to see her. The last time I had seen her was at my own 30th birthday dinner and I wanted to support her just as much as she had supported me. We didn't see each other as much during that time since I had been on the road and she was now the mother of a beautiful little girl, but we always took the time to catch up with each other from time to time via phone.

The day of her party, I had managed to eat some toast and take a shower, but by the time I was ready to begin getting dressed, I felt so tired and dizzy that I had to lie across the bed until I could regain my strength. When I woke up, it was the next morning. Too embarrassed to call Kellie, I told myself that I would just call or stop by when I was in a more cheery mood. I never wanted anyone to see me in a bad mood, but many times I was too tired to fake it. I couldn't make up for not coming to her party, but I was sure that since she was so popular, my absence would be overlooked.

About two weeks later I received a rush of calls. Kellie had been found murdered in her new condo as her daughter slept in the other room. No one has ever been convicted of taking my friend away from me, away from her parents, away from her daughter. She was gone. The one person that I always remembered as being one of my first true friends, was gone. Just like Mamma T, I never got to tell her how much I loved her for accepting me for me. The one day that I had the open opportunity to show my love, my body had given out before I could walk out the door. I began to realize just how short life could be.

The day I bought my glucose meter, I began to cry while walking down the aisle and looking at all the diabetic products. Just driving to the corner store had worn me out physically and when I got home, I cried some more as I tried to figure out how to use the new device that I would now have to keep with me at all times. Just as I wiped the tears of self pity and took a deep breath, my phone rang. I was laid off that Friday at 5:00 pm. Great, I didn't have health insurance anymore.

I literally gave myself fifteen minutes to cry as much as I wanted to. I didn't make it past eight minutes. It was time to move. So I did. Within two hours of the bad news, I had already written up my "Get Back in the Game" Plan. Part of my plan was to start back with the projects that I had started, but never finished. If I was going to be unemployed for awhile, I was going to be the busiest unemployed person anyone could find!

I first had to do some spring cleaning and doing so, I found a few journal entries I had written on through the years. They reeked of depression and insecurity. The confusion of existence filled the pages. If I had not been there myself, I would have mistaken the journals as suicide notes. It was hard to believe that even though I had been living my life successfully and somewhat under my own terms, that I still had some rooted issues that had festered throughout the years. As strong as I thought I was, there were still areas of weakness. I looked at myself in the mirror. Were these feelings from the same smiling girl in the mirror? Who was she and how could a girl that looked so happy, have so many stories of feeling so alone? How could I have lived my whole life with her and not have taken the time to listen to her cries?

The Light Bulb Turns On

Soon after that, I began reading the book *Queen* by Alex Haley. That was the start of something tugging at my spirit. I would go out to places and would see mixed kids with their parents and I wondered if they'd be writing the same journal entries one day. Not if I could help it. They had to know that they were ok. Alex Haley's grandmother, Queen, had spent most of her life trying to find her way in life between color lines. I had already spent thirty years of mine. Life is too short to battle such identity issues for so long. I couldn't let the next generation go without having a better head start than we did. Although we figured it out along the way, it doesn't make sense to let the issues fester over time.

My book had to be complete with all the things I wish I had known growing up. It had to answer the questions that I asked about growing up, but was too afraid to ask. It needed to be a reference point for issues that the average person doesn't go through, but it also had to include those issues that most young adults are curious about. After all, we're still human, just like everyone else. It had to talk about the issues that were found from studies on biracial teens, but were never confronted head on.

It angered me that the books available on raising biracial children fell into only one of three categories. One category of books dealt with the experiences of biracial people and their parents. I found these books interesting in the different cultural scenarios that occurred, but I couldn't find any *solutions* rooted in these fascinating stories.

The second category of literature was self-help books for the parents of biracial children discussing different methods of parenting in order to preserve the child's full heritage. These books are a great resource for parents that make it their duty to give their children the best parenting, but again, where could I find answers for myself on who I am? This question led me to the third category of books.

After reading about others' experiences and the parental advice, I stumbled upon the third category of books that were studies based on the psychology of mixed races. Most of the studies were done using focus groups on the west coast of the US where the culture is a lot more diverse than where I grew up. Living in the South where I had witnessed Ku Klux Klan rallies blocks away from my college dorm and attending a high school where some of the white girls quit the dance team because they didn't want to dance with us black girls, studies of biracial children aren't quite as advanced. The families in those focus groups on the west coast surely weren't from the same environment I knew of.

Who Will Step Up?

What I did discover from the research were the issues of identity and how they affected biracial young adults. The psychology of how a person is raised and how that reflects their self image was interesting because it dealt with where the problems lie for biracial kids. I then began to understand the importance of the self help books for parents on raising their biracial kids. Growing up, these tools weren't available to my parents and they still did an incredible job, but I can now appreciate the resources that are out there.

Many of the studies related the lack of self identity to more serious issues later on in a person's life. I was surprised to hear of the alarming rates of substance abuse and evidence of low self-esteem in biracial teens. The tales of depression, behavioral problems and drug or alcohol abuse, all stemmed from the need to fit in somewhere. Some of these issues began to sound familiar. But just as I read on about the findings, the books ended. There was no happy ending, no solutions to the problem. Not even a suggestion.

We've come so far, but where do we go from here? If it has been such a profound issue, enough to write books on, why hasn't anyone done anything about it? The statistics of problems added to the statements that biracial people are one of the highest rising population in America were scary. Is this what we want our future rising generation to look like?

Parents and counselors talk to teens about staying in school and saying no to drugs. Modeling schools make a fortune from teaching kids how to look confident and poised. Why can't someone talk to biracial young adults specifically about these same issues that have been proven problematic? If they had the time to do research, why not look for a solution too? Don't label us with a statistic and walk away leaving it up to us to figure out on our own. Passing us over as "other" is how we've gotten to the point we're at now. No one ever recognizes the "other" category. Who wants to deal with that? They've figured out the how's and why's, but when are they going to talk about what to do about it? Do we need to wait another twenty years for that too?

I'll Do It

Being mixed doesn't mean that our mixture of races will somehow save us from the common blues. Everyone faces life challenges. Sometimes though, I don't think the world really understands the inner conflicts that we don't speak about. These inner conflicts are often overlooked as normal growing pains. What they don't realize is that these inner conflictions are more than that awkward puberty phase of self identity. Some of the issues that biracial children go through carry on far past their teen years. The truth is that there are a few factors in life that are just a given to most people, but the normal cultural activities of a family somehow become skewed when there is another set of cultural ideas in the same household.

I am the proud daughter of a German mother and African-American father. As a brown girl, growing up in the South with a Swedish name and a southern accent (and a lisp when I speak), I give credit of my understanding of self to my diverse upbringing from *both* sides of my family, yet I remember vividly, many life lessons learned on color lines.

What it taught me is that at the end of the day, no one will remember me as a German girl *or* a Black girl. They will remember me as the person that I was to them. That's where my focus should lie. What difference will I make in the lives of others? Sometimes the only thing you have to give is what's inside of you and believe it or not, that's really all you need. So here I stand the voice of a girl who may not have all the answers but is willing to share what she's figured out so far.

It's Your Turn

The information in this book comes from my own research and real life experiences. In this book, it's my hope that I will be able to show other young people who are biracial or multi-racial, that despite their difference in appearance and set of various cultural backgrounds, they are still full of purpose and opportunity.

Within this book we'll talk about the life principles that come with living a fulfilled life despite the odds. Because biracial kids have an additional set of issues to face, I'll show you how I've dealt with my issues of insecurity. There's a lot that I've learned about myself and I know that you will too.

Once you complete the book the work will then begin as it will be time to start your own empowerment within and self discovery. I'll ask you a few questions about your own experiences. Take the time to think about these questions and write down your answers. We all have a story to tell and most of these questions are the ones that I had to answer for myself leading up to my journey of what you're reading right now.

Afterwards, I want to hear from you! Don't just watch the movement, join the movement. Empowering within comes from our individual power and spreading it within our own community. Feel free to send me any journal topics that you care to share so that we can collect our stories and share with each other. Each of you have a different story to tell that's all your own and someone out there needs to hear it. Doing so would be *your* first step in making the difference in someone's life by showing them a part of who you are.

You can post your responses on the website, or email me. You can use your real name or make up one; it's totally up to you. I just want to hear from you!

My website, SwirlPower.com is also a great resource for the latest news and products that I recommend as well as a place for you to give me your feedback on the questions from the journal section. Think of it as our own site to relate, respond and empower each other. The website address is *www.SwirlPower.com*.

So let's get started in defining what it means to have that *Swirl Power*!

What "They" Say about Kids like Us-as If It Really Matters

The overwhelming result in most studies claim that *not all*, but *many* biracial teens deal with the issues surrounding a lack of self identity which can lead to self-hatred, alcohol and drug abuse, suicide, and depression. According to these studies biracial kids often lack the testing skills for academic achievement while struggling with behavioral issues both in school and in the home. While it often gets looked over as simply a rebellious stage, these issues actually affect kids like us well into our adult years. It's alarming to hear these statements because it's often setting the tone of who we're expected to be before we get a chance to prove ourselves otherwise. These types of statistics are what drove me to the journey of writing this book.

Literary and Psychological Theories

What struck me as being very odd is society's acceptance of these beliefs as being simply a part of our chemical make-up. It's funny to see how the underlying belief that mixed people somehow have a tainted blood line that keeps us from being considered normal human beings. Here are a few examples of how scientists and literary artists have portrayed us in the past, starting back in 1912.

➢ In 1912, French psychologist Gustave LeBon contended that "mixed breeds are ungovernable."

➢ Charles Benedict Davenport in his article entitled "The Effects of Race Intermingling" in 1917 stated his belief that "One often sees in mulattos an ambition and push combined with intellectual inadequacy which makes the unhappy hybrid dissatisfied with his lot and a nuisance to others."

➢ American sociologist Edward Reuter wrote in 1931 that "the mixed blood is [by definition] an unadjusted person"

➢ In the 1950 novel by Elizabeth Coker, *Daughter of Strangers*: "The idea of the mixed river of her blood was whirling in her brain and in her troubled, uneasy frame of mind she had become a stranger to herself."

➢ In 1978, during the study of the mulatto in American fiction, the "tragic mulatto" character is often cast as irrational, moody and completely tormented by his or her "racial disharmony," "clash of blood," and "unstable genetic constitution," typically dying while still young.

The Ugly Side of Human Nature

In any social setting *any* minority group is going to be looked at and labeled as immoral and uncivilized by the majority. The term "different" usually goes on to refer to those that are misfits to society. To add to the separation, color lines are then drawn within that community again where social status is drawn by one's color complexion.

In terms of family, intermarriage within the same culture is considered the norm and any deviance from that is considered immoral and rebellious. This is often true in cases where the intermingling occurred while the men were away during war or exploration. In most cases, the women and their children were shunned by *both* sides of their families. This is often the story in Asia where children were born of US soldiers and the local Asian women.

Recognition Without Recognizing

There has been an increase of attention on the life challenges of biracial people over the years -particularly after Tiger Woods became popular in the 90's. Before then, biracial people were recognized, but not in terms of their issues. As I said before, it wasn't until the mid 90's, when I was old enough to drive, that I even had a name for what I was. The term "mixed" was also used to describe hybrids of dogs and I had refused to use the word as much as I refused to use the N word. It's a shame that the racial issues of biracial people didn't really seem to be much of a topic of discussion until we began excelling in a sport dominated by wealthy white men and holding high positions like our President Barack Obama.

But even with the recognition of the issues, we were still taken lightly-and still are. Just this morning I read a post from a biracial guy announcing his appearance on NPR to discuss being biracial. Excited to hear the interview and what others had to say about the topic, I scrolled down to read the comments posted by subscribers. Instead of encouragement, I saw comments about "the two zebra boys" in the family photo that was posted and questions on where the "baby daddy" was. There were several comments about the black and white dog ironically being in the picture. One comment even stated that they were tired of biracial people wanting too much attention and that biracial people should just accept racism the same way that other ethnic cultures accept them. Needless to say this didn't sit too well with me.

I have a lot of theories about the issues of acceptance that we face and it doesn't stem from any outdated psychology or biology. What it boils down to is the sheer ignorance of just not knowing, mixed in with normal social behavior. The people that are confused about us are speculating that we're the ones in the state of confusion! They then take what's different about us and make it into something that lowers our social status in order to make them feel more superior.

As a woman, the most disturbing statements are those that stereotype biracial women as sexually promiscuous, out of control, and as one writer put it, "ruled by their passion." It's also assumed that attractive biracial women are vulnerable and rely on their looks to get by. In sadder cases, Amerasian (American and Asian) women in both Vietnam and the Vietnamese-American community have very few job options. Seen as racially different and the product of assumed prostitute mothers and worthless fathers who abandoned them, they're sometimes labeled as sex objects and are sexually abused.

Family Matters

My theories are backed by family studies where research shows that the key to a child's understanding of self lies within their family roots. At an early age, we become the most comfortable in our skin when we're with our family. It's there that we are surrounded by people that look like us and share similar family values. Most of our identification comes from our family.

When a child can't identify *physically* with their parent, the parent can't be that reflective mirror for them. The sense of emptiness and abandonment makes them feel as if they never quite belong. The puzzle piece fits, but it's the wrong color. They feel as though their existence throw's off the overall picture of what a family should look like. In some cases where the parent remarries to a spouse of their own culture, that child only sees life in the world of those parents- especially if the other biological parent isn't present in their life.

We Just Want to be Accepted

With all of the historical studies, it's clear to see that feelings of rejection and being singled out are contributing factors to rebellion and depressive behavior. In a society hungry for acceptance, no one wants to feel like they don't fit in, but in the case of biracial kids, they're automatically singled out. Once we step out of our house, we become the walking question mark.

I think one actress said it best when she described how her mixed heritage has been discussed when her agent tries to book television work for her. As her Asian and white heritage is simply a product of her parent's love story, in the entertainment industry, her Caucasian heritage makes her the "diet" version of an Asian. The more subtle variation of Asian characters makes her more accepted than the full on version.

Cultural and Identity Barriers

More recent studies have been focused on the actual behaviors of mixed race children as they relate to common social behaviors of young adults. In these studies, conclusions have been drawn that biracial and multiracial kids typically have higher rates of behavior issues and psychological disorders than their peers. While these studies take a close look at teens, I think we can all agree that those years are what help lay the foundation for who we become as adults.

Especially in areas of rural, less diverse communities, the subject of mixed race becomes an issue that others can't relate to. The children of recently immigrated family members that have strong cultural ties to their homeland, can be caught in the cultural web of their family's traditional culture versus adapting to the culture of their current surroundings. Also within their close circuit of loved ones, some biracial people struggle with others' theory that they're being disloyal to their ethnic heritage and even to the point of somehow coming off as socially superior. In some cases, the lighter complexion, the less they're accepted as being full-blooded.

Along with the rejection within close quarters, when out in the world there is the battle against society's racism against them. As an example that I relate to, racial slurs are thrown out to biracial people, even if they have a white parent. Many young men are pressured to be like the men of color portrayed in the media in which stereotypical images often lower their expectations of achieving a higher social status. For men of African-American heritage, the assumption that they are suppose to be a "gangster" limits these young men to reach out to be the best that they can be. The media plays the same mind game for young women who are bombarded by sexual images. These types of images make them feel as though being sexy and provocative are the only ways to be admired. Both of these myths are easy to believe especially if you're talking about a kid that is looking for a mother or father figure in their life. They're looking for acceptance by any means possible. Without the right guidance and exposure, these young people go through the most exciting years of their life thinking that their respect from others can only come from being a celebrity, video vixen or criminal.

We're Not Mentally Unstable, We're Mentally Discouraged

Confusing nature with nurture is where all this so-called research has totally missed the boat. Biracial people aren't mentally tainted because of their mixed blood; they're *mentally discouraged* by society's racism and ignorance. Being mixed isn't the issue; it's the misunderstanding, racist culture that we live in that's the problem. This same culture doesn't understand us nor do they accept us as being of equal value. We're considered only half of this or half of that. Because they don't quite understand us, they expect us to not know either. It has only been ten years since we began having the option of choosing more than one race on the US Census. When that option was available in 2000, almost 7 million people in the US claimed their multi-racial heritage. It makes me wonder as I look at the copies of the census reports of my ancestors from ninety years ago. How much more would I have been able to know about who I am had they had those options? My grandmother was born in an area where Native Americans and blacks became their own culture, but without that key ingredient, I will never know where that part of my history began. I know it's there, I just don't know where.

From the theories of "mixed blood" being considered tainted, to all of the confusing environmental factors, mixed race people often get a bad rap for never being enough. According to the rest of the world, mixed people are never considered enough to be a true person because we're only *partially* conscience of who we are.

Don't Judge Us by Our Blood, Judge Us by Our Lives…You Know, Like How You Do for Everyone Else

As a result of being labeled the redheaded stepchild of society, emotional isolation leads to possible depression and substance abuse as a way to cope with our feelings. That same judgmental society then labels us as misfits and categorizes our repression as being mentally disabled. But instead of placing behavior issues under the category of mental disorders, try looking at the leading factors. Lots of people get depressed and succumb to alcohol and drugs to deal with their feelings, but does it start out with their bloodline? Of course not. It stems from life's experiences that somehow lead a person in the wrong direction. Why would anyone think differently for people of biracial heritages?

Passing Us Over Simply As "Other" Doesn't Fix the Problem

With no solutions to the obvious issues of the high rates of substance abuse, depression and isolation, the open wound goes untreated for biracial people. Perhaps there's no solution because no one cares as long as it doesn't involve them personally. Maybe it's easier to write it off as just being the way of the world. It's much easier to look over the issues of those checked as "other." When has that category ever been recognized for anything? It's more like an "etc." No one ever goes back to the "etc." to get the details on what that actually consists of.

Well I'm tired of being just a passing thought. It's time to address the real issues at hand. No more sweeping things under the rug. We can't afford to do so. We're losing lives to drug and alcohol abuse, HIV/AIDS and suicide and these are issues that, believe it or not, can be avoided. Besides, with biracial people being one of the fastest growing groups in the world, it's time to do more than pass over the issues at hand. Barack Obama, the president of the most powerful country in the world is biracial. I don't know what other hint the world needs!

We Can't Leave It Up To "Them" To Figure It Out For Us

We can no longer let society sweep our value under a category that never gets noticed. Accepting what's set before you is suicide in itself because it's putting trust into the hands of a stranger. If you leave it to society, you'll be locked in a padded room and misdiagnosed as genetically invaluable before you can give yourself a second opinion. Instead of becoming a statistic, it's time to be an example. Let's leave the guessing game to a society still trying to chase down a man named Bigfoot and some creature called the Loch Ness Monster.

Just because you're mixed doesn't mean you have to be confused. Confusion comes from simply not knowing. You may be different, but you're not dumb. If you know who you are and what you're worth, there's no room for confusion. Educate yourself *on* yourself. Take this time to study the most important subject and be ready for the test. Being different is simply a part of your greatness and greatness comes with moments of testing –a test of faith, ability and wisdom.

Only *you* have the ability to know who *you* are so don't look for any fraudulent professors to help. Don't take the subject of YOU lightly. Study yourself from the inside out. Learn who you are. The study of yourself will be the most exciting course of your life and it starts now.

We may be different, but there are some things that people can't take away from us. No mixture of blood or society's opinion can take away our entitlement to willingly think for ourselves and expose our minds to everything that's out there for us to absorb. There are no barriers if you don't look for them!

It's kind of like how I used to sneak into exclusive events. I would pretend that I *was supposed* to be there. I'd hold my head up high and walk into an elevator just as calm and confident as I could. Most times I would do so without even thinking of a backup plan just in case I was questioned. From red carpet events to corporate Christmas parties, I've yet to be questioned simply based on my own refusal to be denied-mentally. Doubt yourself and it's bound to show on your face. Once it's on your face, the world will see it.

Besides looking the part, there are some key life principles that go along with it all. Looking confident is one thing, but being confident in who you are is a completely different beast because it comes from within. There's no set formula in getting to that point in life as it all evolves over time, but just to kick start the process, the following chapters contain some of the life lessons that I've learned along the way. Take each principle and strive to work harder in each one for your everyday living. Although you've probably seen them before in passing, we'll take a look at how some of them relate to you as being of mixed cultures as well as simply being, well…human.

I Am Filled With Purpose

For a long time, I never quite understood that I actually had a purpose. I was told that I was good at doing certain things, but I never saw them as having much value. It wasn't until later in life that I was able to connect the two together. While understanding that being filled with purpose is just the beginning of living the life you've always wanted to live, it's also the last thing that you'll be able to see results of. It takes an entire lifetime to really see the fruits of your labor. That's because it needs time to grow.

So what does purpose look like and how do you know when it's right in front of you? Since purpose isn't a tangible object, it's often strived for, but still overlooked. Wherever you see talent, over time you'll be able to unwrap that talent to find it's outlet of energy called "purpose." You see, the day you were born, you were delivered as a package of purpose. Nothing on this earth is made without a purpose.

Nothing. Even dirt has a reason for existence.

The trouble that we have with purpose is that since we can't physically see it, we treat it like a fairytale. We hear people talk about it and we support them by celebrating it, but we don't believe that we can find the same thing for ourselves. It's as if Cinderella took the one and only pumpkin ride available.

What Is It That You're Really Envisioning? People often mistake fame and fortune as their purpose. Our purpose isn't for other people to love and adore us. Loving and adoring you doesn't change people's lives-it doesn't change *anything* actually. It doesn't bring world peace or some noble recognition. We all have a talent in one way or another. You're talent isn't your purpose either. It's what you do with that talent and how you use it to serve others, that helps to fulfill your purpose. Never mistake your dream to be all about you. If you choose to do so, you'll miss the whole point of a purpose. Purpose is about sharing your gifts with others in a way that makes their life better. Purpose is all about enhancement to what's already there. If things were meant to not have a purpose, our creator would have made everything perfect from the start with no room for improvement.

As you go through life, your experiences bring out your natural gifts and talents. It's in these qualities given specifically to you that you'll find your life purpose to be fulfilled. The power of knowing that you're filled with purpose helps you to do several things:

➢ It keeps you focused on nurturing your gifts and talents. Then you begin to understand that every experience and challenge endured is simply boot camp for living out your own purpose.

> It keeps you from being envious of other people's success. When you understand that everyone's purpose is catered to their own destiny, you can look at their success as proof that purpose really does exist.
> It uses the things you are passionate about in order to help others. You'll find part of your purpose hidden in any desire that you have that is for the benefit of others.

Your creator made you to go through your own experiences–both the good and the bad. No one wants to read a book that's all about happy stuff and neither is anyone's life. Not only were you destined to go through challenges in life, you were also created to have both strengths and weaknesses. Your strengths allow you to fulfill your purpose while your weaknesses remind you that you're human by giving you something to work on. All in all, your strengths and your weaknesses both help to fulfill a purpose throughout your lifetime. Your entire life has a storyline of joy and sorrow. Within it all, the story is filled with tales of growth and challenges. All of these things make up what comes together as an amazing history book called "you."

Where There's Purpose, There Also Lies Responsibility

No matter how long it takes for you to find different aspects of your purpose, they're definitely there. We all find those strengths and talents at different times of our lives and once we recognize them, it becomes our responsibility to turn them into purpose. It doesn't just happen and it's not always what we expect. If that were the case, everyone wouldn't be born with their own. We would just have to pick one out of a hat, draw straws or something.

The first thing you need to do is get over yourself. Stop thinking that the world owes you something or that you should be sitting around being admired for being who you are. Yes you're gorgeous to look at, but the world is full of beautiful people. Yes you're smart, but the world has a ton of geniuses walking around. You may be one of the greatest athletes, but no one holds the number one title forever. Get over yourself and start digging into what your real purpose is in life. Until then, continue to go through your life's experiences so that you find your strengths and predestined victories. Along the way, you'll find that just as you have more than one strength, you'll also have multiple opportunities to use your given purpose. Yes, your purpose comes in a very large package!

Just because I'm mixed doesn't mean I'm confused because I know that all of my life lessons and the things that make up who I am, are in line with the reason for my existence.

I Know Who I Am and the Legacy That I Carry

There's no feeling like the confidence of being able to tell a stranger who you are and what you represent. You carry a legacy within you that was built upon a foundation of sacrifice and hardship. You're no mistake and you're no passing thought. From the day you were born, you were given a purpose and a plan for your future. Not only that, but you were also born with a history. That plan for your future is better known as your destiny while that history you were born into is called your heritage. One of the most amazing things about you is that you're here. You're the direct result of the lives of your ancestors, proof that life carries on time after time, after time. The mere fact that you're able to read this book is evidence of efforts made by someone in order to teach you how to read. But having an appreciation for being able to live on this earth is one thing, knowing what has transpired before you were even thought about, is another.

In my 8th grade language arts class we were given the assignment of designing a poster that described the origin of our name and how it represented who we are. I was one of those students that actually got excited about assignments like that. Anything that didn't involve a book report was pretty cool to me. I just didn't see the need to report on the same book that the whole class had read together just to prove that I was in class. Wasn't that what taking attendance was for? We all knew what happened in the end so why should I have to report on what you already know?

As the teacher explained the homework assignment, I prepared in my head all of the cool magazine pictures I could cut out for my presentation. I had lots of to pictures to choose from. Mom had subscribed us with *Ebony* magazine and had kept pretty much every *National Geographic* magazine since the 70's. I had a thing for learning about far away countries and traveling to distant lands just from browsing the magazines. I even memorized the words to *We Are the World*, so if I did get lost in a faraway country, I would at least have one song I could sing with the natives.

My teacher began showing examples of how other students had displayed the meanings of their names…hey, wait a minute, I thought. You mean names actually have meanings? Besides the Matthew, Mark, Luke and Johns of the world, I had never thought of names actually having a meaning to them too! -and if so, what the heck would "Svenya" mean? Shoot, my mom had already Americanized my name from the proper spelling of Svenja to Svenya just so people wouldn't mess it up-although most did anyway. Now it was supposed to mean something too? Oh boy. I think I'd rather write a book report.

I guess my concern and confusion showed on my face as I looked around the room. There was only one other person that I was *sure* who's name probably didn't have a meaning either. I'm still not sure if I ever pronounced his name right. That boy had more syllables in his first name than any word I had ever had on any of my spelling tests. Eventually, he went by the first syllable of his name, Sly, but I couldn't even do that. If I had done that, I would have been giving myself the boy version of my name, Sven. I couldn't win.

As my teacher pulled the two of us to the side to give us an alternative assignment, I was kind of embarrassed. I almost felt as if I was being punished for not knowing who I was and too stupid to even know why my parents had given me such an unusual name. Either way, I made it through the class that semester without having to stand up in front of the class to admit that I didn't know who I was.

It must have been the experience that was meant for me to bear because that summer my mom and I traveled to Germany where I saw my name on a souvenir item for the first time. Oh my gosh, I was so psyched! Up until that point, I never knew that my name was actually a common name-in Sweden anyway. Since then, I've gone on to learn about my family's history on both sides of my family along with the origin of both my first and last name. My father and I have researched our family tree back eight generations. Through the internet, we've found US Census reports, death certificates and military documents. My aunt helped us put together some pretty interesting information and we didn't stop there. After digging up those roots we've been able to meet some of our long lost relatives and since then, have started a three year tradition of holding our annual family reunion.

Before that point, I had never experienced a family reunion –or should I say my own. I mean, I've snuck into a few -but they weren't my actual family. (Yes, confidence will even get you into places where people forget that they don't actually know you!) Every year we go to an old church that sets back in a wooded area. The story of how it all came about is pretty amazing.

On the border of North Carolina and South Carolina lies a huge tourist spot called *South of the Border*. Any traveler driving down I-95 in either of these states will see the tacky billboard advertisements for this place. As corny as they are, people always remember them. The actual site isn't much to look at as it's pretty much a small run down amusement park filled with souvenirs, motels and over-priced gas stations. Although it's not the most exciting place to bring the family, by the time you drive past the fifty billboards on the highway you feel as if you *have* to stop and experience this place. I'm not even sure the amusement park rides are still in operation, but then I still don't understand the giant dinosaur and sombrero characters either. There's no overall theme to this place. Just stuff.

One day as my father was driving past the exit of the locally famous hot spot, he got off and found himself taking a side road. It all looked so familiar to him, but he wasn't sure why or where he was exactly. He came upon an old church in the woods. As he drove up the dirt road, he recognized the church as a place he had visited many times as a little boy. As he walked towards the graveyard next to the small brick church, he was approached by an older lady.

"Can I help you?" she said.

As my dad explained his somewhat familiarity with the place, he mentioned the names of a couple of deceased relatives just to see if they rang a bell.

She began to laugh.

"Did I say something funny?" he asked.

"Yes, I know them. Follow me," as she walked up to the tombstone of my dad's great aunt.

The memories began to flood through his mind as he realized that this was the very church that his Aunt Lizzie had taken him to years ago. From that day forward, he has made a point to learn as much about our family history as possible. As he says, "My grandson won't know where he came from unless I tell him."

Through Daddy's research, he began to get in touch with other relatives to piece all of the family history together. That's when he met his cousin Ruth who incidentally, lived twenty minutes from my house. Since the reunion of our family, we've held our annual family reunion to connect with each other and we always end the weekend with church service at that very same church. On our first visit to the church, Cousin Ruth let me know just how significant the church was to my family. She also remembered the church. It was the same church that she had visited fifty years ago at her mother's funeral.

Believe it or not, the history of my family didn't stop there. Through our research, we found that my family's history was rooted more than just soil deep at that church. The land that the church and the tourist site all sat on was once owned by my ancestors whom eventually sold it to the family that had built the tourist attraction. I now drive through that area with my chest stuck out as I try to imagine what it would have been like back then. I appreciate the wooded smells and corn fields that are too tall to look over and I wonder what my ancestors were like. What type of trials did they have to go through while living in the South as a colored family with more land than most whites, being treated less than human? What kind of hard work did they have to endure in order to be so successful? How much of their endurance do I hold within me?

On my mother's side of the family, I know bits and pieces from what my aunt has dug up. Because of the distance and divide of much of my mother's family, there aren't any family reunions going on. I don't think that's even a familiar concept to Germans. I have heard some pretty interesting stories from my mom about a great great-grandfather who was a world traveler and who had sailed around the world. There are stories of relatives marrying several times, changing their names and stuff that would be more interesting than a James Bond movie.

My mother was left in the hands of a few relatives while growing up so her sense of independence has grown within her from a very young age. She talks of her first experiences to the United States from Germany and all of the culture differences that took some getting used to, like how she couldn't understand why Americans would greet her with "How are you?" but never stopped to hear her answer. The more she talks of her crazy adventures, the more it sounds like my mom would actually have been cool to hang out with back in the day!

Stories like these keep our heritage going so that every generation knows about who they are and where they come from. Wouldn't you want your grandchildren to know about you? It's more than simply knowing who your parents are and where they're from. It's about knowing the bloodline of those that have survived the struggles of fighting for freedom and equality and their stories during political and religious wars. These are the stories that make world history more personal to us. No matter where your ethnicities lie your ancestors made some serious sacrifices to make a life for their family and for you. Whether you're adopted or your parents never married, your stories may vary from others, but there's still a story. A story of how you came to be. When you're fortunate to have more than one ethnicity in your immediate history, you have the responsibility to learn of those struggles so that you can pass down those stories to the generations to come.   Not only must you know who you are, but you have the responsibility to carry the legacy on and represent those that have endured the struggles that have afforded you the life that you live today. Every ethnic group has a struggle. You have the advantage of seeing more than one perspective on life through several different struggles.

It All Starts With A Name

One of the most interesting differences in cultures starts with the naming of a child. While many Latino families name their children after someone special such as a relative, some cultures allow a close friend of the family to choose the baby's name. In some religions, it's common to have children named based upon biblical characters. Other religions such as Judaism and Hinduism may hold a naming ceremony once the child is born.

However your name came to be, it's like your second skin. As part of knowing your purpose, do the research of the origin of your name. How did your parents come up with it? Where does your last name originate from? Get to know that person in the mirror by finding out how their name came to be.

Climb That Family Tree

There are lots of resources to help you find out the names of your ancestors. My favorite is *ancestory.com* because they allow you to research outside of your country and they may be able to find legal documents as well. I have a copy of my great, great grandmother's death certificate. It's interesting to see the names on old census reports and to read about what their occupations were. I even noticed that all of the records of my relatives were marked that they were able to read. That's a big deal for African-Americans growing up in the South soon after the ban of slavery! That alone, gave me confirmation that I come from a legacy of educated relatives far beyond my grandmother. Just more confirmation that I have the responsibility to represent their wisdom.

Put those researching skills to use. Talk to your family members about your family history and do your own research. Learn the language and the customs of your cultures. Take the time to compare the differences in cultures and how they vary. You'll find a greater understanding in why you go through traditional rituals and you'll have something to talk about with others. Part of your purpose is to expose others to the wonderful world of you.

Know a Little History of Swirl Around the World

Being mixed also adds on the responsibility of educating yourself about the different instances where mixed race people have blossomed over time. To pinpoint the beginning of mixed races is impossible simply because it has gone on since the early ages of time. Although I won't go into all of the possible mixtures of ethnicities, it's important to realize that whenever there is cohabitation of more than one group of cultures in an area, the mixture is bound to occur, thus, the beauty of being biracial or multiracial. It can happen in any point of time in history in any place.

The United States of America

Today, through the immigration of cultures from all over the world, the United States has the most diverse population in the world. As diversity continues to grow, the integration of cultures grows as well. It is estimated that thirty to seventy percent of African Americans are multiracial; virtually all Latinos and Filipinos are multiracial as are the majority of American Indians and Native Hawaiians.

Interracial marriage, especially between whites and blacks, was deemed immoral and illegal in most states until the first half of the twentieth century. Similar laws in California and the western US prohibited white and Asian American marriages as well. However, the US Supreme Court overturned this law in 1967 in the Loving v. Virginia decision, which overturned all remaining anti-interracial marriage laws in the US.

Native Americans in the US and South America

Within the Native American culture, the social status is traditionally determined by one's ancestors with the highest statuses given to those of the least amount of Non-Native American blood, thus the term "full blooded Indian."

Long ago, there was a lot of cohabitation among Native Americans, Europeans and Africans, resulting in a population of mixed bloods. At that time the term mulatto was used to describe these people with mixed heritages. It was later studied that after cohabitating in the same areas, especially in the Southeastern region, the Native-Americans and Africans began intermarrying. As a matter of fact, it happened so much that it's said that thirty to seventy percent of African Americans today have partial Indian ancestry. So why don't they know this? Because at that time, there was a law called the One-Eighth Rule which stated anyone with an eighth of African blood, was declared Black and if you were *any* percentage of Black, you were forced into slavery and other civil injustices.

For those populations of Native Americans that survived being ousted by the White settlers, (as many as ninety percent of most tribes died from diseases contracted by the Europeans) many of them reestablished their homes in parts of the Southwest and as far south as Peru and Mexico. There they integrated and intermarried with the Spaniards so much so that by the era of the Civil War the president of Mexico was elected, Benito Juarez, a full-blooded Indian.

The Immigration of the Asian Culture to the US

Prior to 1850, very few minorities migrated to the US from their homeland. However, from 1850 to 1892, the demands for laborers in gold mines and famine in a southern city in China called Canton, brought about 20,000 Chinese immigrants to the western US (that's about the number of the fans at Staples Center in LA for a Lakers game). Fueled by labor competition, anti-Chinese immigration acts arose while Japanese immigrants seized the opportunity. The rise of Japanese workers also fell prey to immigration laws in 1907 and 1908 when they too were coerced to limit the number of laborers coming into the United States.

The Immigration Act of 1924 gave quotas to each country as to how many immigrants would be permitted each year per country. This act was written by Europeans giving them the largest quotas such as 26,000 for Germany and 65,000 for Great Britain. Eastern European countries such as Italy and Poland had relatively small quotas of 6,000 per year. Most Asian countries however, were assigned a quota of only 100 and most of these assigned slots were reserved for whites that were born in Asia.

But there was one loophole. Since 1898, Filipinos were considered American nationals up until the legislation laws in 1930 which allowed them unlimited access into the United States. However, once the loophole was sealed shut in 1930 the quota was set to only fifty per year. It is even documented in subsequent laws in 1935 and 1939 offering Filipinos free passage *back* to the Philippines.

The term "Amerasian" was coined by the author Pearl S. Buck from her novel *East Wind, West Wind* in 1930 and is often used to describe children of Asian mothers and American fathers. Additionally, the term "Eurasians" is often used to describe those of both European and Asian descent.

Contrary to popular belief, the first African Americans in the United States were not slaves. In August of 1619, twenty blacks arrived in Jamestown, Virginia and were indentured servants just like most of the white immigrants. The first black child born was William (no last name recorded) in 1623 or 1624 to his parents, Antoney and Isabell.

Through the worldwide demand for sugar and tobacco and the development of gang labor, in order to meet those demands, white Europeans looked for a cheaper way of getting the job done outside of indentured servants. They tried to enslave Native Americans and other whites, but their attempts failed. Native Americans were far more familiar with the land and were noted as being very sickly under the conditions of slavery. White servants were protected by a recognized government and could blend in with a crowd if they escaped. However, Africans were strong, sometimes said to be worth four Indians, and visible by their skin tone. They weren't protected by the law and they were bought at a cheaper price without the option of freedom. The same money that could buy an Irish or English servant for seven years would buy an African for their entire life under the slavery laws. For 400 years, Africans were sold into slavery into the land we now call the United States of America.

After the Emancipation Proclamation in 1863 slaves were freed, however the interbreeding of slave owners and their slaves had already begun. This resulted in thousands of "mulatto" slaves, the product of slave owners most often violently sleeping with their slave women. Again, the amount of biracial children born was never accounted for because of the One-Eighth Rule forcing mulatto children into slavery.

Vietnamese Immigrations after the War

After the First Indochina War and under terms of the Geneva Accords of 1954, many of the French troops took thousands of Vietnamese wives and children while about 100,000 Eurasians stayed in Vietnam. Negotiated by both countries, France offered Vietnamese Eurasians the opportunity of citizenship and an education at the age of 18. Many Vietnamese Eurasians took this opportunity and later sent for their mothers to join them in France.

Later, after the US's fight in the Vietnam War in 1975, 30,000 Amerasian children were left fatherless in a culture where the father is the symbol of the household. Therefore, they were looked down upon amongst their own people. Without a voice to empower them, they continued to struggle as they fought immigration laws in order to come to the US. But once on US soil, they struggled to adapt to a new culture. Unlike the French had done in the Indochina War, the United States did not recognize the children of the US soldiers born and these children were somewhat forgotten. Some historians say that the overlook was due to the severed ties with Vietnam. Others come to the conclusion that the US government immediately directed its attention toward refugee resettlement and the troops that were still missing in action. Another explanation suggests that because Vietnam was the only battlefield that the US didn't emerge victorious from, the US simply wanted to forget that it ever even happened.

The Filipino Movement to the US

After the Spanish-American War in 1898 and the defeat of Spain, the Philippine Islands as well as other remaining Spanish colonies were ceded to the United States in the Treaty of Paris. In 1946, in the Treaty of Manila, the US recognized the Republic of the Philippines as an independent nation although the US maintained as many as twenty-one military bases and 100,000 US personnel. After 1992 when the bases closed, it's estimated that as many as 52,000 Amerasians were born throughout the Philippines.

On US soil, the mixture of Filipino and Native American heritage is often hard to notice upon first glance. This is often the case in California where the darkness of skin is assumed from the purity of Native American blood, without the knowledge of Filipino heritage. You can also find the Filipino culture in Hawaii where immigrants traveled in the 1840's during the push for plantation labor.

The Multiple Cultures of Hawaii

It is believed that the Hawaiian Islands were first populated by the Polynesians from the Marquesas and Tahiti somewhere between 300 and 500 CE. Following the cultural growth, Europeans arrived centuries later, around 1778 when British explorer James Cook arrived. After his publication of several books about his voyages, European traders and whalers found the islands to be a convenient location and source of supplies.

Unfortunately, their arrival also brought small pox, measles and influenza, killing a fifth of the Hawaiian citizens much like the spread of diseases that caused the deaths of Native Americans on the US mainland.

Chinese workers settled upon Hawaiian shores in 1789, followed by the first legal Japanese immigrants arriving in 1885 also as contract laborers for the pineapple and sugar cane plantations. Shortly afterwards came Puerto Rican immigrants after a natural catastrophe wiping out the fertile lands of Puerto Rico. A wave of Korean immigration occurred between 1903 and 1924 and again around 1965. With such a high worldwide demand of these supplies, plantation owners maintained control of the financial institutions, allowing them to continue importing cheap foreign labor for their gains.

Other groups of ethnicities also joined the islands such as Samoans, Mormons, Fijians, Gilbert Islanders, Norwegians, Spaniards, Germans and Russians. Besides the Portuguese and Japanese who frequently migrated as a family, most of the laborers that were imported in were young men and therefore most likely married within the local community of women.

Today, Hawaii's highest percentage of citizens is Asian American with lineage from the Philippines, Japan, Polynesia, China and Korea. Other mixtures of culture link to Mexico, Puerto Rico and European countries like Germany and Ireland. Hawaii is also the birth home of US President Barack Obama who is of Kenyan and Caucasian descent.

In Hawaii, the term *hapa haole*, meaning "half Caucasian" is used to describe those of half-Asian of Chinese, Japanese, Korean or Filipino ancestry and half-Caucasian descent. On the islands, those mixed with Asian, Polynesian and European are most often described as *cosmopolitan* or *local*.

India

The mixture of Indian and British descent is often referred to as Anglo-Indians. The origination of the estimated 600,000 offspring dates all the way to 1616 when British traders began trading goods with India. The British Raj period in India lasted for over 130 years before the British left. During that time, British soldiers married or had affairs with Indian women and now many of the Anglo-Indians are living in India and the United Kingdom.

Sri Lanka

The island of Sri Lanka has a long history of being a settlement of various ethnicities from all of over the world mainly due to its location. Located in the Indian Ocean, many traders settled there and intermarried with local women. Three major multiethnic groups are still present as a result.

The Sri Lankan *Moors* can trace their ancestry from Arab traders and live primarily in urban communities, preserving their Arab-Islamic cultural heritage as well as some Southern Asian customs.

Burghers are considered Eurasian in which Portuguese, German, British and Dutch settlers intermarried with the women of the land. Still a small number of Eurasians also descend from Swedish, French, Norwegian and Irish ancestry.

The third group, the *Kaffirs*, descend from the 16th century Portuguese traders and the African slaves with whom they brought with them. The Creole based language was very distinct and dance style such as Kaffringna and Manja still exist today.

Singapore

As of September 2007, the population of Singapore was 4.68 million of which almost half were people of multi-heritage, including Eurasians and Chinidians (of Chinese and Indian heritage).

Singapore became a British trading colony after the European control of the Malaysian area in the 16th century. It was later the site of one of Britain's most important naval bases. Malaysia itself was formed in 1963 when Singapore and the states of Sabah and Sarawak joined the Federation of Malaya. However, Singapore left in 1965 to become a separate nation.

In this part of the world you will find cultures of Malaysia, China and India. Intermarriages between the Chinese and Indians are the most common. The number of Chinindian children is hard to account for since the government only classifies children based upon their father's ethnicity, which in most cases are Indian.

It is here that we see a great example of how religious beliefs play a huge part in the mixture of cultures. It's uncommon for Malays, who are predominately of the Muslim faith, to intermarry with either the Indian, predominately of the Hindu faith, or the Chinese who are mostly Buddhist and Taoist. However, it is very common for Muslims and Arabs to take local Malay wives since they share a common Islamic faith.

United Kingdom

According to reports, Britain has the highest rate of interracial relationships in the world and is expected to have the highest growth rate of ethnic minority groups by 2020. It is estimated that 1 in 10 births are that of biracial ancestry. Most of the multiracial citizens use the term "mixed" to describe themselves. The minority cultures mixed within the majority European includes African, Asian and Caribbean.

By the 1920's there were several settlements of mixed race populations largely due to the British seaports such as Liverpool and Cardiff. There, many visiting African and Asian seamen were introduced to the area and later settled in other cities such as London, Nottingham and Manchester.

Canada

In Canada, you will find various combinations of minorities including Black and South Asian, specifically in Toronto, followed closely by White and Black, White and Latin American, White and Chinese and White and Arab just to name a few.

South Africa

Multiracial South Africans are commonly referred to as "coloured" which is ironically, an outdated term used in the US to describe minorities. The second largest minority, right behind the white South Africans, Coloureds have descended from the African culture and Dutch colonization.

In South Africa, the Prohibition of Mixed Marriages Act in 1949 prohibited marriage between whites and non-whites. This was an apartheid law that was later repealed during the presidency of P.W. Botha in 1985. The apartheid legislation in South Africa was a series of different laws and acts used to enforce the segregation of different races in order to cement the power and dominance by White Europeans over the majority people, black South Africans.

Mestizo (mixed) as commonly described, are the multiracial people of South America making up a large portion of the continent and even the majority in some countries such as Dominican Republic, El Salvador and Belize. Such unique combinations of cultures have existed and have always been acknowledged since colonial times.

In Brazil, most Brazilians identify themselves as multiracial. Although the term "pardo" is used on official census, it's typically not used by the population, who call themselves "moreno" in terms of light-moreno or dark-moreno. Since multiracial relations in South American society have occurred for so many generations, it's very difficult for people to trace their own ethnic ancestry. However, if traced back thoroughly, most will find a history of Sub-Saharan African, Portuguese or Amerindian in their family tree.

As you can see, the mixture of cultures reaches far beyond what our eyes can see and the beauty of it all is that it shows us our strength in numbers as a whole. We're more than just a category called "other." We're a representation of the world's diversity. We're the legacy left by explorers, soldiers, international businessmen and the strong women that endured ridicule and pain. We represent life. We represent love. We represent humanity-and that's nothing to be confused about.

Just because I'm mixed doesn't mean I'm confused because I know for a fact that I was born from a royal bloodline of history makers and I am committed to represent the legacy that they've passed on to me.

About eight years ago, I was on a promotional tour in San Antonio. It was a hot summer day and we finally had a day off to relax and do some sightseeing without having to wake up the next morning to head to another city. So far, we had ridden to about twenty-five towns and although we had some great experiences, the crew and I were pretty anxious to just unwind.

My partner in crime was Sylvester. Sylvester and I became two peas in a pod although many times we bickered at each other like two married people who loved to hate each other.

I was about twenty-six at the time and the opportunity to be on the road, away from a desk job and eating out every day, all while getting paid to do it, was a dream job for me. I had never been to San Antonio before and so far the only thing that I knew about the city was that it was a pretty cool and diverse place to be. That and the reality that the sweltering heat in Texas was unexplainable to my friends back home. Even a southern belle like me couldn't understand how it could be so hot but still not considered being in hell.

With San Antonio being so close to the Mexican borders, it's naturally populated with Hispanics. Back home the rise of the Hispanic community had just begun to rise and in a way, I celebrated it. I liked living in a world of more than just black and white with just a few other nationalities sprinkled in between the two. I may not have been able to speak the language, but at least I looked somewhat like them. I had a round face (from eating too much fast food probably), I had tanned into a reddish brown for the summer and I had long dark hair like many of the Mexican women. So there I was in a place where I could pass as Hispanic –as long as I wasn't required to open my mouth. I didn't habla a word of Spanish. So far I had been mistaken as Mexican by several people as they began speaking in a language that made me shrug my shoulders. I felt bad for deceiving them, but I still enjoyed feeling like I was somehow apart of their community.

On our day off, Sylvester and I decided check out the The San Antonio Riverwalk, which is a beautiful, historical site in the city. It's filled with a small river and a walking path (thus, the name Riverwalk) along with hotels, stores and great restaurants. Before we left the hotel, I slipped on my blue jeans shorts and blue tank top. Our tour was sponsored by *Hanes* so t-shirts, tanks, and shorts, we were never in shortage of. We had so many on the bus that Sylvester was actually denied access to Canada when we visited Detroit, in suspicion that he was involved in some kind of t-shirt trafficking.

After a couple of hours of visiting the historical sites and tasting a few Tex-Mex dishes, we decided to head back to the car. It had been a pretty long day already and the heat was becoming unbearable. As we walked a few blocks towards the car, I noticed a group of kids gathered by the bus stop. Hmm, they must be going home from school because they're all dressed in their blue school uniforms, I thought. They looked a little out of uniform though because their shirts weren't tucked in and …wait a minute. It was Saturday.

Great. There I was with my Mexican looking self, wearing all blue and walking towards a street gang. I was only a block away and there wasn't enough time to switch directions. I didn't want to tell Sylvester because I wasn't sure who was behind me and would hear our conversation nor did I want him to panic. I continued on my conversation with Sylvester as I took a deep breath. I felt heads turn towards us and eyes watching me like a hawk. At that point, I wasn't sure if what I was even saying to Sylvester made any sense. As we approached the group, I did what only I knew to do. I smiled. I smiled and I kept rambling to Sylvester as if I had no idea why they were looking at me. Southern charm at its best.

I don't know what was said about me after I passed by and since I don't speak Spanish, I probably wouldn't have been able to understand anyway. They may have even laughed at my naïve gesture, but I didn't care. I even got a smile back from one of the guys. Needless to say, I stopped wearing blue for the rest of my time in San Antonio-and red too for that matter.

Although that scenario wasn't the only time that I've been in the presence of danger, I've always felt a presence of protection around me based partly on my own self respect. While we can't control what the outside world does, there's something that we *can* control within ourselves-our own self respect.

When you respect yourself, you take full responsibility of the value that lies within you. When you give people that same respect, it becomes contagious. You cut through all of the vanity and egotistical drama that people seem to think they have to walk around with. I didn't know those kids. I have no idea what their lives were like, nor did I see the need to judge their decision to join a gang. It was their life and although I don't understand it, I respect it. All I know with full authority are the decisions that I've made for me. I hadn't planned on smiling that day in a way to defuse the situation. I just did what came naturally and showed the same respect that I expected in return. And guess what, I got it back in return.

Here are a few principles that all resort in sharing the respect you have for yourself, with others. Apply these principles to your everyday life in order to help you live by the one saying that stays true in all walks of faith.

The Golden Rule Will Never Get Rusty

The golden rule states that we should treat others just as we'd like to be treated is accepted in most cultures around the world in some form or another. It must be a pretty powerful statement for the world's most wide spread faiths to agree on this overall statement.

"Blessed is he who preferreth his brother before himself." *-Baha'i Faith*

"Hurt not others in ways that you yourself would find hurtful." *-Buddhism*

"Do unto others as you would have them do unto you." *-Christianity*

"This is the sum of duty: do not do to others that would cause pain if done to you."

- Hinduism

"None of you (truly) believes until he wishes for his brother what he wishes for himself."
-Islam

"Thou shalt love they neighbor as thyself." *-Judaism*

Looks like they can all agree on at least *one* issue after all, but what does it all mean to you and how do you know when you're doing just as the passage instructs?

The first clue that you're on the right track is to check how you treat yourself. Every faith refers to how we treat ourselves using phrases like "wishes for himself" and "if done to you." It's here that we recognize that we should be in expectance of the rights given to any human. This passage could have easily spoken of the expected attention given to a king or queen, or of a person in a high political position. Instead, each passage uses our own self as the example. Our position rank, our ethnicity and our financial status has no bearing on who we should use as a prime example. We automatically qualify as the prime example.

The second part of the passage goes on to speak on how we are to treat other people. This takes away the selfish factor and allows us to share the same concept with everyone that we come in contact with. We must acknowledge that they also qualify to experience the satisfaction of respect. Respect can only be given based on the qualifications that you've given to yourself.

Be Honest

I've been working on my honesty in terms of being less concerned of how polite I come across and more focused on saying what's actually on my mind. The problem is that once I'm on a roll, I don't know how to stop. The other day a lady walked up to me in a clothing store and asked, "Can I get your honest opinion?" as she held up two pairs of shoes.

I looked at the shoes and the dress that she had pulled out of a shopping bag. "Well, just how honest are we talking here?" I responded.

"Never mind," she said to me as she rolled her eyes and walked away.

I guess she couldn't handle the truth. I shrugged my shoulders and continued browsing the aisle with a grin on my face. Had she gotten my openly honest opinion, the shoes weren't the problem. It was the hideous dress she was trying to match them with that disturbed me.

Most times we are dishonest with people because we're lazy. Unconsciously, we'd rather be nice than honest. It's much easier to be polite and not say a word, than it is to think about the right way to say how we really feel and then go through the anxiety of having a conversation about it. Instead, we just nod our heads and write it off of no importance of our own.

Part of the reason why small children are so entertaining is because of their honesty. Their honest opinions always seem to make us laugh because they say exactly how they feel with no filter. As they grow up, they become more concerned about how others see them and because of their new concern for their image, they speak less and less about their true feelings. By the time they're adults, they've played the game long enough to know when to just smile and bear it. Ironically, the older we get the more we begin to go back to caring less about what others think and are liable to say anything!

I remember talking to my grandmother for the first time in over a year or two. She had pretty much been in vegetable state with very little communication past a mumble. My dad called me from her bedside so that I could talk to her. I was so excited to finally get to talk to her that I couldn't sit still as I held the phone to my ear. After two years of being in a coma, her first words to me were, "You ain't married yet?" I can't wait to get old so I can say how I really feel and get away with it.

Being honest also runs you the risk of rejection and adversity. This is the part that scares us. No one likes rejection and we all try to avoid adversity every chance we get because we don't want to rock the boat. While rejection is a possibility, it's a possibility that we all have to live with so we may as well stop canceling ourselves out of opportunities based on the fear of rejection and adversity.

Having self respect for yourself and others comes from the daunting task of being honest. If adversity arises because you're honest, it can do only one of two things. It can bring strength to a relationship *or* break up a relationship that wasn't meant to last anyway. Either way the results lie, you've knowingly told the truth and that's what matters most.

I'm willing to bet that ninety nine percent of the punishments I was given as a kid was due to my mouth. I wasn't very mischievous in my actions, but my smart mouth trying to *justify* my actions got me in more trouble than I'd like to admit. Sadly enough, my punisher (my mom) is probably the sole donor of my sassy gene. Watching your mouth and the things that come out of it isn't as easy as it sounds. Even now as I learn to hold my tongue, I often battle with the need to justify my intentions. The problem with saying whatever comes to mind is that in the process we make ignorant statements that we don't really mean. Our first thought is to upstage the other person-often without even hearing everything they have to say.

Big mistake.

Now not only are we looked at as being flat out wrong, but we've said things that are hurtful and can't be forgotten. So how do you effectively communicate your point without being walked over? Try these suggestions a couple of times.

> Stop talking and start listening. There's a lot you're going to miss if you don't. You have two ears and one mouth for a reason.

> Get clarity of the other person's perspective. Repeat back what you heard to be sure that you understand them. Who knows, they may have something valid to say.

> Once you have clarity, be sure that you're just as clear. If you can clear up something that was said by the other person, even better. This is how they know that you're listening to them and if they see that you're listening, they have no choice but to do the same.

What you'll discover is that many times you're both saying the same thing but in different languages. Other times, there's a small piece of misunderstanding which took everything in a different direction. Still other times, you're just dead wrong.

Living in a society that likes to prejudge based upon first impressions makes it important for biracial people to not let others stereotype us into how they expect us to act. I mean, let's face it, most stereotypes aren't positive.

Honor and respect are both harder to gain than they are to lose. You may work to gain these privileges over time, but can kill it all with one wrong move. Oddly enough, everyone seems to think that they *deserve* respect from everyone else around them. Not feeling like you're getting the honor and respect that you deserve? Check what you're giving out first. Not only to others, but the respect you're giving to yourself that others pick up on when they see you. Again, the Golden Rule doesn't get rusty.

Honor and respect from the people around you comes from both how you present yourself physically as well as how you interact with them. If you carry yourself in a way that doesn't show that you respect then you've lost them before even opening your mouth. Open your mouth with ill-mannered, vulgar language and you can forget it. It's just not going to happen for you.

I once interviewed a girl for a job at one of the manufacturing sites I worked with. I noticed her professional attire for the interview although it really wasn't necessary for the environment we were in, but I appreciated her effort to want to make a good impression. When I asked her about her last job experienced, she cursed three times before I stopped the interview. I don't even think she realized what she was saying because it had all become a part of her language. From that point on, I knew that I wouldn't be able to trust her to come in on time and to do the job I needed her to do. Even if she was a good worker, she wouldn't have gotten the opportunity to prove it. Application disqualified.

Some of these issues I link to parenting. The American culture has become too relaxed for kids these days. They aren't held responsible for anything. Yet, the parents allow them to do everything else that is considered adult behavior. They aren't expected to greet adults with a firm handshake nor do they look people in the eyes when speaking. However, they're able to watch R-rated films and own cell phones. They feel obligated to materialistic things as if they have jobs or something. Only some of them know proper etiquette and they only choose to use them on special occasions. Simple respect like saying "yes" or "yes ma'am" are now downgraded to "yeah." A simple word such as "no" has now become "nah" or "uh-uh." They're allowed to speak to adults using the same lingo and street slang as they do with their friends. And the parents wonder why they can't get the respect they deserve from their kids? Where did we lose the value of something so simple?

Speaking with honor and respect are basic rules to interacting with people in an even exchange. One of my favorite books, *How to Win Friends and Influence People* by Dale Carnegie, shows us how to do just that. I'm sure most people are drawn to the "influence people" part of the title, but the overall theme of the book is simply that if you respect others, you've won them over as a friend. Once they're your friend, you've got the power to influence them.

Learn to Forgive

The biggest misconception about forgiving is that when you're asked to forgive, you're assuming that you're being asked to forget. Forgetting isn't that simple, especially if we've been hurt and because forgetting is hard to do when we've been done wrong, we automatically cancel out our willingness to forgive. This happens a lot in families divided by race. For biracial people, stories of rejection by other family members are common and because the rejection comes from someone from our own circle, the hurt cuts pretty deep.

Forgetting may never happen in some cases because of the scars that were left and the damage done. Forgiving is *actually* the opposite of forgetting. Forgiving is about accepting what's real and moving forward while forgetting is not accepting the realities of a situation and pretending like it never happened.

The true meaning of forgiveness is moving past the current feelings of bitterness and considering the fact that one day, you too will be seeking forgiveness. This isn't something that *could* happen or *may* happen. This is something that WILL happen and when it does, you'll want the same fair shot at forgiveness. Part of being human is being imperfect and no one on this earth is exempt from that quality.

I think the one flaw that comes into play with personal relationships and the challenge of forgetting, is that we hold two different standards. We judge others based on their *actions*, but judge ourselves based on our *intentions*. When loved ones act in a way that seems to betray us, we react to their actions. Even when they try to explain what their intentions were, our hearts can only focus on what they did. Oh, but when the shoe is on the other foot, we talk until we're blue in the face about what our intentions were. All the while, the other person is only reacting to our actions-just as we would do. For every action there's a motive. Your questioning should be about the motive first, then the actions surrounding it. There you will find a better understanding and the forgiving process can begin. If there's a situation that still has you in the unforgiving mode, try these suggestions to get to the starting point of being able to forgive.

> Look for understanding. Why did this happen? Ask for the person's intentions. What led up to this point? *Forgiving requires understanding.*

> Learn from others' mistakes while also learning about yourself. What did this person do that hurt me so that I can be sure to not follow the same path? Did I play a part in what happened? If so, what can I do in the future to prevent this from happening again? *Forgiving requires learning how to prevent things from happening again.*

> Move on from it and let it go. Most people don't know or don't care how much you hurt because of their actions. Don't carry that wound around as it will only hinder your own growth. *Forgiving requires work to get past the negative emotions that can rot inside of you and prevent you from living a happy life.*

In the end, forgiving is about freeing your heart up in order to live life with the emphasis on the good rather than the few disappointments that also come your way. We will all be lied to and disappointed by others. It's a part of living. The hurt comes from the fact that these disappointments often come from those that we love. If we didn't love, we wouldn't care. The power of forgiveness though, comes from knowing that we also make mistakes and would look for the same forgiveness.

Just because I'm mixed doesn't mean I'm confused because I display myself as deserving of the same royal treatment that I give out through honesty, respect, understanding and self control.

I Make the Ultimate Decision of How My Life Plays Out

Recently, a friend asked me an interesting question: If you knew a woman who was pregnant, who had eight kids already, three who were deaf, two who were blind, one mentally disabled, and she had syphilis, would you recommend that she not go through with the pregnancy?

If so, you just killed Beethoven.

One thing about being great and full of purpose is that greatness doesn't come from mediocrity. If you show me any amazing phenomenon, I'll show you the astonishing miracle behind it. Beethoven was born into a world of hopelessness. Anyone looking in on the situation would have cancelled him out way before he was even born. We hear stories like this all the time. How people forced into unlikely situations are empowered to do more and as a result they become the great people in history that we read about today.

Being biracial puts us somewhat in the same boat. When we're born, there are family members that doubt our chances in life to succeed. As cute and adorable as we are as children, in the back of their minds, some relatives think of all of the culture confusion we will someday face. Research tells us that we'll be prime candidates for having mental disorders, alcoholism and drug abuse. We're told that we will have issues on knowing who we are based on our mixed cultures. Even within our close communities, we're only looked at as being partially qualified to be a part of the group.

But just as Beethoven, we *aren't* what others see in us. We have the power of making the ultimate decision on how our lives play out –that is, if we decide to take the wheel.

You Don't Have to Choose

I love the food that my Caucasian family cooks because it's always so healthy. I love the food that my Black family cooks because it always tastes so good. Now why should I feel the need to choose between the two? What does that solve and why should I have to choose which makes me happier? Shouldn't it just matter that I'm happy?

I don't get it. It doesn't make sense to me. So I don't choose.

Living between more than one culture gives us options. Options that most people don't get, nor do they ever realize are available. In a monoracial family, some activities are somewhat the norm, but imagine the possibilities in a household with more than one idea of fun. There are just too many holidays to limit ourselves to just a few.

What I appreciate about my family is the fact that they never made me choose and I was never made to feel as if I were partially a family member; even in my extended family through my dad's second marriage to Mamma T. And although my mother's family once rejected her, the extended family members in Germany have welcomed me into their lives.

During the holiday season my immediate family always celebrates a traditional German Christmas which is held on Christmas Eve. As kids, my brother and I were escorted upstairs to our room where we would wait until we heard the sound of an angel's bell. Once we heard the bell we would come downstairs to a beautiful pine Christmas tree lit up by white candles and decorated with silver foil tinsels. The entire living room smelled of pine.

In order for us to receive our gifts, we first had to give some type of performance to the group. I think some of our guests only came over for the cheap entertainment. We would have to recite a poem, sing a song or play an instrument. Afterwards, we were able to open our presents one at a time while taking turns. Yes, our Christmas celebration was very orderly. While other kids were lying sleepless in anxiety for Christmas morning, we were busy playing with our new toys until we passed out from excitement.

After Daddy remarried, Christmas Day became a world tour of house visiting with family and friends. It was then that I realized that we were the only family that celebrated Christmas the night before. Before then, I couldn't understand why the neighborhood kids were still in their pajamas when we came by to check out their new toys. I also couldn't figure out how Santa Claus knew to come to our house when he was busy in Germany too. But when my brother explained to me something about a time zone I just went along with it as if I understood what he was talking about. He had a way of scrunching up his eyebrows when he spoke that made me feel as if what he was saying was really deep and if I couldn't understand, then I was just a total idiot.

Choosing only one culture to be associated with is like limiting your options and refusing to have two Christmases. Who would want to do that? Refusing to choose puts the power back into your hands to discover all that you carry inside of you. You don't have to choose and no one has the right to choose for you.

Limiting Our Options Is Only Keeping "Them" in the Dark

The funny thing about people is that they always want to know exactly how they should categorize you. On first glance, they want to be able to read everything about you to find out what they have in common with you. When evaluating this commonality, ethnicity always seems to be a part of the deciding factor. Your ethnicity gives others a point of reference. A lot of times the inability to categorize us by a certain ethnicity puts others in an uncomfortable position because they lose that point of reference.

The issue that I take on with mainstream society isn't their inquiry; it's the lack of options given to us. They lay out the options to choose between *this* or *that*-but only according to *their* list. That's not right. Even dogs get the privilege of being introduced as a mixed breed of some sort. Do you know what they call a dog mixed between a labrador retriever and a poodle? A labradoodle. Now how can you say *that* with a straight face? But they want us to claim only one ethnicity? That's all we get? I've seen more options in a box of crayons!

Now, would I like for anyone to combine both my ethnic backgrounds into a new word like how people butcher Brad and Angelina into Brangelina? No thanks. There are enough made up words circling around us already. I've got a whole list of nicknames we've been given. We're not some kind of caricature.

To be honest with you, I'm still getting used to the word "mixed." The first time I heard my god daughter use the word "mixed" to describe a person, it kind of struck a nerve with me so I asked her to say "biracial" instead. It reminded me of how people describe dogs. Even though she was only about ten years old and didn't mean anything by it, I didn't like the way it made me feel.

On the other hand, it's just a sign of the times. I'm sure it's just as much of an adaptation that my grandparents had to make from being called Negro, to Black to African-American. The only difference is that many years have passed between the times the term "mulatto" was used to describe us and now, when the terms, "biracial," "mixed" and "multiethnic" have arisen. Between the mulatto phase up until now, there really hasn't been a name for us. There was no gradual transition from one term to another. New descriptions just began showing up after a couple of decades. I just happened to be born during that time of non-existence.

Now that us "others" have a name, I'm hopeful that people will begin to adapt to our diversity instead of making us choose whichever would make *them* more comfortable. I think it's possible. But first they have to get out of the mindset that the only thing that makes sense is what's familiar to them. That's the issue that I think will take some getting used to.

Over time, a look at the US Census shows the growth of diversity. In 1870, the U.S. Bureau of the Census divided up the American population into races of White, Colored (Blacks), Colored (Mulattoes), Chinese, and American Indian.

In 1950, the census categories grew to: White, Black, Hispanic, Japanese, Chinese, Filipino, Korean, Vietnamese, American Indian, Asian Indian, Hawaiian, Guamanian, Samoan, Eskimo, Aleut, and Other. Although more nationalities were added, it also included the "Other" category for the first time. This is where we got dropped off in the box along with everything else that didn't quite fit their mold. It was either the "Other" box, or we had to choose. Pretty ironic how the acceptance of diversity grew, but the acceptance of the diversity in one person was simply put in the box that got ignored.

It wasn't until recent years that multi-ethnicities were included on the census allowing persons of more than one race to have the option of stating so. Up until the year 2000, the US Census never really looked at the number of multi-racial people and boy, were they in for a surprise when they did! After the push for more options on the census, it's reported that almost *7 million* people reported that they were of more than one ethnicity. That's almost the size of the population of Hong Kong! And that only includes those that participated in the census that live in the US!

Up until recently in the US, a biracial child of any set of heritages was only documented as one. If the child had a parent of brown skin, that was the noted ethnicity documented. Because of this disregard, the statistics of the US regarding race are very conservative when quoting the actual number of biracial children born so we honestly don't know exactly how many biracial people have been born. The world is just now opening its eyes to see how strong we are in numbers and the numbers keep rising as biracial Americans have been reported as being one of the highest rising ethnic population.

My Short Attempt to Swirl with a White Boy

With part of my heritage coming from the Anglo persuasion and since I'm so "down with the swirl," often times people ask me if I've ever dated a white guy. My response is, "Well, I tried."

When I was about thirteen years old, I had a slight crush on a white boy at track practice. He wasn't on the track team, but he lived close to the high school track so he would come over and watch the girls. I'd like to think he was just coming to see me, but at that age I'd be fooling myself. After asking for my phone number several times I finally gave it to him.

For a couple of weeks we talked on the phone about all the stupid stuff that thirteen year olds talk about-absolutely nothing of importance to say the least. I could tell by the things he described about his hangouts and friends that he was pretty much a black guy in a white boy's body. In fact, most times I forgot about his skin color until I saw him at the track. Just as I was easy to spot out in my dance class, he stuck out like a sore thumb too. It was as if the "spot" light was so bright that it had lightened him into his pale complexion.

One afternoon while on the phone with him, I heard his mother in the background mumbling. I paid it no attention as I seemed to have the same phone interference when I spoke on the phone around my mother. As we continued on in our meaningless conversation about tennis shoes and the latest radio mix he recorded on his cassette tapes, I heard a woman pick up the phone.

"Get off the phone. Now!" his mother said. I had heard that tone before so I knew she wasn't playing.

"Uhhh..Do you want to call me back?" I asked just to ease his embarrassment.

My mom had the same type of habit of picking up the phone and using her deep voice as a scare tactic to let me know she meant business.

"No, just hold on," he said as he put the phone down.

At that point it was just she and I on the phone. Neither of us said a word as I held my breath. I heard him in the background from her receiver as he yelled to her to put the phone down.

Looked like he was going to be on punishment for awhile, I thought to myself.

In the middle of my thoughts, I hear him say, "But she's only half black! Her mamma is white!"

What did he just say?

"She's what? Hold on." she said, and she gets back on the phone. "So exactly what are you honey?" she asked me.

I sat in silence. I had heard the question before, but this time it was different. It was coming from a place of hatred. If I had said that I was white, I'd hate myself for it later and I surely would never be able to meet her in person. If I told her I was black, she'd probably hang up on me. So I just beat her to the punch. I hung the phone up.

I couldn't believe what I had just heard. I tried to erase my memory and fill it with a made up conversation. That's the problem with cordless phones, they make you hear things that aren't really said. But if he did say that, did he think that he was defending me by pulling the white card or was he defending *himself* as if me being half white had qualified me into his world? And what did she mean by "So what are you?" I was an honor student that played the flute, an alto in my church choir and I enjoyed playing tennis, basketball and dancing. That's what I was. Her son on the other hand, skipped school to hang out with his friends to do nothing all day. She should have been honored to have me as a positive influence for her son. What was I? I was a lot better than she tried to make me out to be. That's what.

About twenty minutes later, my phone rang again. "I'm sorry about that. She makes me so sick! She hates it when I talk to black girls."

Was that supposed to make me feel better?

"That's cool. Well, I gotta go." I said as I hung up. And that was my stint of dating a white boy.

How to Answer the Question: "What Are You?"

Would I ever date outside of my race? Of course I would if I found the right person. But I haven't. What stuck with me through that experience wasn't his race, it was the question of what I was, but that certainly wasn't the first or the last time I've gotten that question.

If you ask any multiracial person about the most common question they get asked, you will get the same question: "What are you?" It's become so common in our dialog that we can even detect when the question is arising.

On introduction, we are the only class of people that are required to explain our existence and because no one else has to experience this, they really can't empathize with how it makes us feel. The power of answering this question goes back to our overall message which is to take this common scenario and turn it into another opportunity. This is yet another opening to introduce the uniqueness about you. You've just been given another chance to be more than just your name. Think of it as them asking, "Why do I get the sense that you're very special?" Now the "spot" light is on and the conversation begins. When you think about it, it's actually a great conversation starter. Here are a few phrases that I use when being asked, "What are you?" Feel free to use any one of these and be sure that you say it with pride.

"I'm (insert ethnicities). What made you ask that?"

"My mother is from (insert ethnicity) and my father is from (insert ethnicity). What would you have guessed?"

"Do you mean, what's my nationality?"

"Well, I'm from (location) although my family roots are (list nationalities). And you?"

"Well, do you want the long version or the short version?"

"I'm Human. What are you?"

"Pretty."

However you answer the question, the ultimate secret of answering is to be sure that you're not choosing from *their* list of options like a multiple choice question. Smile and tell them exactly who you are. If you don't know who you are, how do you expect for others to even care? If you have an unusual name, find a way to help people remember it. Don't be offended. In some cases, people that you meet haven't been exposed to a spectrum of names from different nationalities. I often tell people that my name is "Svenya, it rhymes with Kenya, but sounds like an S-W at the beginning of it." Then give them the opportunity to practice their new word for the day. Don't be afraid to correct them if they say it wrong. I'm sure they'd correct you if you mispronounced theirs, wouldn't they?

The age old question of who you are will be asked of you throughout your entire lifetime. As annoying as it can be at times, seize the opportunity to introduce yourself- your *amazingly unique* self, to someone new.

Depression, Diabetes and Grandma Panties

Part of growing up is finding our own way in life. Our purpose and our identity aren't written on our birth certificate so we have the daunting task of figuring it out on our own. Those of us with mixed DNA are no different. We are all in the same search. The difference is that during our years of self discovery, we're also dealing with self identity as it pertains to our race. This can be a pretty rough period of insecurity. Those insecurities often follow us through our young adult years where during rough times, we go back to those familiar feelings. They tend to show up in ways that we don't understand and at a time that's least convenient to our confidence.

Make no mistake. There will be times in your life when you feel like a complete failure, times when you just ask, "Why am I here?" There will also be times when others seem to have all the answers to your life's confusion. There's not one human on this earth that doesn't have doubts and fears and in that sense, and you're no different. But just like everyone's life experiences are different, so are the ways that we learn to find our own way.

I can remember three separate occasions when I hit really low times in my life. The first time, I was down on my luck. The second time around, I was in search of purpose but was too full of sorrow to figure it all out. By the third occasion, I had totally been worn into a state of depression. I had taken all that I could take and my body was now unequipped to go on. My relationship was in shambles, I was laid off from my job, I had lost one of my dearest friends to an unsolved murder case, I had gained weight and my body was in a pre-diabetic state. I no longer had a reason to get out of bed in the morning and when I did, my body wanted to collapse. To relieve myself from it all I just didn't get out of bed. And believe it or not, this is where the story begins!

Depression is an illness that affects the entire body including your thoughts, moods and behavior which most often can't be willed back together. The unrealistic thought by those that suffer from depression is that the feelings are based on their own failure. While the exact cause of depression isn't known, the contributors are thought to include chemical defects in the brain involving *serotonin, norepinephrine* and *dopamine*.

Medically, there are two types of depression. The two types of depression are *dysthymia*, the most common which is a chronic non-disabling type of depression, and *manic-depression*, an extreme switch from depression to extreme elevations of moods. Patients with dysthymia depression suffer from many symptoms of depression although they don't reach the established criteria for a diagnosis of depression. Manic depressive patients are somewhat rare, in which a person goes from one extreme to another. They may be very energetic one day and fall into a deep depression soon afterwards.

In every low occasion, I dealt with my sorrow in the same way. I ate. Even when my money was funny, I never missed a meal. Had I ended up homeless, I would have been the first to volunteer at the soup kitchen. I even dated a guy simply because he always took me to *The Cheesecake Factory*. He was ugly. He was rude. But he fed me well.

Trying to go through life while being in a state of depression is the loneliest feeling in the world. It's as if you're walking around with a cloud surrounding you. You are conscience of what's around you, but you can't hear anything and no one can hear you. Even if you cry out, your voice is on mute. When you add illness on top of the depression, it feels like you're walking around with someone on your back. Even going up a flight of stairs is a challenge. Add on another layer of unemployment and heartache and it's a wonder how I was able to stand up straight.

My daily woes included all of the signs of depression: I was fatigued. I couldn't concentrate or make clear decisions. I felt hopeless. Nothing seemed to bring me joy, including the activities that I once enjoyed like dancing. I suffered from insomnia only to switch over to oversleeping. I had gained weight. My body ached and I suffered from constant headaches. Quite simply, I was a total mess.

As I look back at that period in my life, each issue was so entangled with the others that it was hard to focus on just one at a time. Most people that are going through depression don't know how to get off of the merry-go-round. It's not because they don't want to jump off, they just don't have the strength to and they're too dizzy to focus on the exit off.

As I said before, this is just the beginning of my story- my story from just a year ago. As I write to you today, I'm just a year away from what I just described.

You see, being in a state of depression is just that, a state. It's a circumstance, a status, a condition. It doesn't have to be a permanent state. I never sought help from a doctor for medications-but then how could I? I didn't have health insurance to cover it. Instead I self-medicated myself the only way that I knew how. I prayed. I cried. I walked. I read. And most of all, I decided it was time for me to get bolder in my requests on what I wanted in life. There were some changes that needed to be made and it started with me qualifying everything that I did. Everything that I included in my life had to make sense. The things that I ate and how I spent my time were the two major areas that needed pre-qualifying. I was the only one that had authority of how my life was going to be played out. No more waiting for a miracle, a man or a new job. Besides, in the state that I was in, I wasn't in the best condition to handle any of those anyway.

I tossed out my sleeping aides to help with my insomnia and traded it for an afternoon walk to get me to the point of exhaustion before bedtime. Those afternoon walks doubled into morning walks as well. I used my walking times to collect my thoughts and focus on what my body was saying to me. Some days were easier than others, but I learned to have patience with myself. The more I included walking into my daily routine, the more my body started responding in a positive way. In the beginning, a thirty minute walk resulted in two hours of rest on the couch and a four hour headache afterwards. As much as I wanted to quit some days, I continued on. Every time I wanted to skip my walks, I thought about my friend Shannon who's an overachiever in everything she does. She once said to me that it's when you do what you don't want to do, that makes all the difference. So I did. Because of her motivation, I was able to increase my walks to an hour and suddenly my rest time decreased to only thirty minutes. It wasn't an everyday occurrence, but the more I kept at it, the more frequent they became. I hadn't lost any weight, but I found a sparkle of hope.

As therapeutic as walking was for me, I began to see that there was room for even more change. As I began to feel the muscle development in my legs and stomach, I decided to take myself to the next level by pre-qualifying the foods that I put into my body. After years of eating out while on the road and coming home just to eat more processed food out of convenience, it all had taken a toll on me. The dates at *The Cheesecake Factory* didn't help any either. I had gone up three dress sizes, but it wasn't the size that was the problem. It was the nauseous feeling that I felt after eating each meal. Eating was supposed to be gratifying, not regretful. Something wasn't right.

Because I have never had much self-control with food, I refused to diet. Dieting would have been a lost cause because quite honestly, I just love food too much. I still love *The Cheesecake Factory* and we have too much history together to just break up. However, I did begin to pre-qualify the foods that I ate. I focused on foods that came from the earth's surface such as fruits and vegetables. I began reading food labels when I shopped in the grocery store. Staying away from ingredients such as high fructose corn syrup and most processed food helped me make better food choices.

Even when I thought I was eating right, my Aunt Rita showed me something that blew my mind. While eating grapes, she showed me that even though I was eating fruit, they were seedless. If they're seedless, how are they able to reproduce? Even the fruits and vegetables had to pre-qualified so that I didn't eat what she calls, "hybrid food" which obviously have been altered by chemicals. Once I realized that food has to do *something* once it's in your system, I began consuming foods that would only do something *good* for my body.

Since my commitment to determine my own destiny, I've lost the fifteen pounds that I gained during that dark period in my life. I no longer need to check my glucose levels and that sparkle of hope has turned into a ray of light. I never knew anyone to beat diabetes until I met me. It took me getting to know myself and my value in order for me to break the habit of letting my body suffer the consequences of my actions.

Accepting depression, diabetes and obesity has become a part of society's norm so much so that we forget that they're also preventable. Ironically, the drug and diet supplement industries are multi-billion dollar companies making money off of people's laziness and insecurities. When you don't have the money to invest in these items, if you stay focused you'll see that all it takes is the ability to start qualifying!

Fighting Depression and Suicidal Thoughts

Because depression is one of the qualities associated with the psychological studies of biracial people, I want to give you some of basic information associated with it. There are also other resources on the SwirlPower.com site, but for the sake of conversation, use the following suggestions if you feel as though you're going through your own dark period in your life. Understanding by educating yourself should be the first line of defense when fighting depression. The more you understand that your symptoms are part of the disease and not personal failure, the more you will be able to work through the process to recovery. A few important factors when fighting depression include:

➢ Patience with yourself and realization that recovery takes time.

➢ Understanding that pessimism and other symptoms will gradually fade away.

➢ Get help from a therapist if it gets too much to bear. They can help you to get well and stay well. The therapist may also prescribe an antidepressant medication while treating your symptoms if they are severe.

➢ Avoid setting difficult goals with deadlines or taking on difficult tasks until you begin to feel better.

➢ Write down priorities and break down large tasks into smaller ones.

➢ Avoid isolation by remaining involved with people and activities that you enjoy.

➢ Keep a regular exercise program which affects the levels of neurotransmitters in the brain, effective in managing depression. Most therapists will recommend this as your first action to get better. I suggest it before using any medications.

➢ Keep family and friends involved in your recovery.

If suicidal thoughts begin to build up, remember this:

➢ *There is ALWAYS another solution, even if you can't see it right now.* Many young adults who have attempted suicide and survived say that they did it because they mistakenly felt there was no other solution to a problem they were experiencing. At the time, they could not see another way out – but in truth, they didn't really want to die. Remember that no matter how horrible you feel, these emotions will pass.

➢ *Having thoughts of hurting yourself or others does not make you a bad person.* Depression can make you think and feel things that are out of character. No one should judge you or condemn you for these feelings if you are brave enough to talk about them.

➢ *If your feelings are uncontrollable, tell yourself to wait twenty-four hours before you take any action.* This can give you time to really think things through and give yourself some distance from the strong emotions that are plaguing you. During this twenty-four hour period, try to talk to someone – anyone - as long as they are not another suicidal or depressed person. Call a hotline or talk to a friend.

➢ *If you're afraid you can't control yourself, make sure you are never alone.* Even if you can't verbalize your feelings, just stay in public places, hang out with friends or family members, or go to a movie – anything to keep from being by yourself and in danger.

Above all, don't do anything that could result in permanent damage or death to yourself or others. Remember, suicide is a *permanent* solution to a *temporary* problem. Help is available. All you need to do is take that first step and reach out.

Trust Me, I'm No Genius

I truly believe that my experience with a learning disability has been more of a blessing to me in the end although it took an uncommon path to get to where I am today. When I think about it, it's still mind boggling because there were so many things that could have been avoided.

My path was a little different than most others with a learning disability because I didn't even know that I had a learning disability until I became an adult. Ironically, I worked for five years at my university's office for students with physical and learning disabilities. At the time I struggled with my studies, but only chalked it up to my busy schedule and the acceptance that I just wasn't as smart as I thought I was. While in grade school, I was forced into set study times. They were very short study times that only required enough effort to review what was learned in class. My dad would even wake me up at 4:30 in the morning to review for my tests.

But in college I was responsible for my own study habits and I was failing miserably at it. It wasn't that I didn't make time to study; it was just the infrequent times when my mind would stay focused enough to put forth the extra effort to remember the information.

After a couple of years, I learned to stroll through the library for awhile in order to clear my mind. The quietness calmed me. Afterwards, I would settle down into a small study room with no windows. After about fifteen minutes of setting up, I could begin working, but only in a way that worked for me. It was frustrating for me to know the hours that I would put into my studies, would never quite help me to ace a test, but the more I began dedicating myself to my own learning practices, I could see my own improvement.

Dancing presented the same type of problems for me. Memorization of the dance sequences was always a struggle for me, especially since I was also battling against being nervous during performances. What got me through was the constant repetition during rehearsals and my own mental rehearsals before I went to sleep at night. To be able to memorize the choreography while keeping your body inline and facial expressions together is a lot to pull off. Not to mention that you have to actually enjoy doing it too!

I can remember in my favorite advertising class, we were given the assignment to read *Ogilvy on Advertising* by David Ogilvy. I was so excited about reading the book that I read it three times and studied it like my life depended on it. When it was time to take the test, I left the auditorium crying. I ended up with a D+ on that exam and I felt defeated. It was the first time that I had ever thought about switching majors. If I couldn't pass a class that I was the most interested in, what good was I in any other class?

As horrible as I felt at the time, I still didn't consider that maybe it wasn't just my study habits. Instead, I just worked harder. I can laugh now at it all only because I got past it on my own and as a result, I'm built stronger. Because I didn't know I was disabled, I never had the opportunity to blame my performance on my disability. Not only did I have to work harder to stay focused, but I learned some of the greatest lessons on organization and responsibility. I learned that everything must begin with organization; knowing what needs to get done and having a game plan of how to get it done. And it grows out of responsibility; keeping myself accountable for every single task without accepting excuses. In the end, my determination trumped my disability.

As an adult, I've kept my disability somewhat of a secret because there's no sense in making excuses for it now. Can you imagine what it's been like to even write this book? My goodness! Every small distraction and random thought can interrupt me at any given second. (Did I leave the hall light on?)

What has gotten me through is the ability to keep my workspace organized and away from distractions while keeping my responsibility to the finished product. What's my purpose and what does it take to get there? The rest is just fluff.

Look for those answers to the bottom line and you're on your way to determining how your life is to be placed out. Life consists 10% of what happens to you and 90% of how you react to it. After a lot of practice you will start to form habits to get you over the humps.

What these so called studies on biracial people with possible mental illnesses forget to include in their reporting is that most people go through trials such as these. There's no set profile for depression, learning disabilities, or health issues. They're nothing new. Even Beethoven went through a period of depression-and that was after he lost his hearing! The only difference is that many biracial people don't always have the same type of support system. It's assumed that if we look okay that we are okay. We're sometimes expected to put on these masks of exotic beauty, but what's behind us is so much more.

Commit to learn about who you are so that you can boldly show the world the purpose that lies within you, despite the challenges that you are bound to face. Whether it's a disability, feelings of self doubt or your health, no one knows you better than you- and why should they? Only *you* have the power to change the circumstance. Never leave that valuable responsibility up to anyone else that most likely can't answer the same questions for themselves.

Just because I'm mixed doesn't mean I'm confused because only I have the right to choose my path in life. I don't have to choose my identity nor will I allow others to decide it for me. I can overcome all obstacles and use them for my path to fulfilling my purpose.

I Treat My Body as My Temple

There are lots of different names for a place of worship; a synagogue (Judaism), basilica (Roman Catholic), cathedral (Catholic, Anglican), church (Christian, Anglican, Roman Catholic, Episcopalian,), kingdom hall (Jehovah's Witness), meeting house (Christadelphians, Mormons, Latter-day Saints), colop (Hinduism), mosque (Islam), derasar (Jainism), daoguan (Taoism) or a fire temple (Zoroastrianism) just to name a few.

No matter what our religious backgrounds are, they all contain a place of worship so for the sake of conversation, I'll use the term, "temple" to include them all. While the religious practices and beliefs may vary in each building, they are all considered to be a sacred place. Once you enter the doors, you enter a place of sanctification.

When we hold our bodies to the standard of a temple, we're committing to apply the same rules that are used when we give respect in our places of worship. I love the way Julia Roberts puts it in the movie, *Eat, Pray, Love*. She says, "God lives in me, as me." If this is so, I take full responsibility of treating my body as the precious temple that it is because it's where my Creator lives.

Your body is also your temple because it's where *you* reside. Your purpose, your strength, your heritage and everything else that you have to offer, is carried everyday in your temple. Therefore, you should make serious decisions on what goes on in and around your temple. Today we live in a world where people tear down and destroy their bodies without taking time to think about what they're doing to their temples. They spray paint calligraphy and puncture holes all over the temple walls using tattoos and piercings. They misuse their temples as if it can never fall and they let anyone and everyone, use it for whatever they please. They voluntarily destroy the temple that they've been given.

As I learned how to take better care of myself, I too had taken part in destroying my temple in the past. Without the proper maintenance, my temple had become weak and ready to crash in. It wasn't until I got to the point of being close to disaster that I decided to reconstruct. The one deciding motive for me was the realization that I will only get one temple, the one that I have.

Qualifying What I Feed Into the Temple

Battling the attacks that tried to overcome my body was an all out war. Just when I thought I was gaining ground, I still couldn't get back the total strength that I once had. The will was there, but the fight had wilted away. I regrouped by refueling myself but I could never get the strength I visualized in my head. It was then that I realized that I had been poisoning myself.

Eating regular meals is part of daily living that we take advantage of. We take for granted that food is readily available and for many of us, there's lots of it to choose from. We're very fortunate. With all of the choices that we make however, we don't always make the *right choices*. We eat out of what's convenient and what satisfies us visually. Pre-packaged foods line up our kitchens and when we go out, we're eating foods from the restaurants' kitchen of the same pre-packaged foods. As a result, our bodies respond to our mistreatment through illnesses and obesity. We then feed medicines into our bodies which causes another set of side effects. The medical commercials seem to list more side effect warnings than the features of the product that are supposed to make you better.

The food consumption cycle is really quite simple; Food enters the body, the body takes what's given in order to function and then it spits the rest of it out. But what happens when the food we eat contains things of no use- and what about those things that are actually attacking our bodies? The body doesn't have a voice and it can only react to what it's been given in order for it to be heard. Not only that, but the body doesn't care if you spent ninety-nine cents to feed it or ninety-nine dollars. It just does the job that it was built to do.

Once my body began to react to the foods I had been eating after years of abuse, it began to talk to me through pre-diabetic conditions and obesity. *What people tend to forget is that diabetes is preventable!* And guess what, so is obesity-if you work hard on giving your body the right fuel to survive. I had been exercising for years, but it wasn't until I started pre-qualifying what I fed into my temple that I began to see just how strong the pillars of the temple really stood.

The Potentially Deadly Side Effects of Being Biracial

Outside of eating right and our mental health, there are attacks on our temple that have been said to be serious issues of biracial people. According to psychological studies on biracial teens and young adults, we have some of the highest rates of behavioral issues and substance abuse. We've been labeled as victims of low self-esteem with many of these behavioral problems as our answer to dealing with it. While these statistics certainly don't reflect us as a whole, I think it's important that we take a look at the potentially deadly side effects of being biracial so that we know what we're up against. While we'll go over some of the heavy hitters, I also have available other resources on my website to check out for further details.

Everyone Doesn't Qualify to Enter the Temple

STD's are sexually transmitted diseases that are mostly spread through sexual contact. With the rise of STD's and unplanned pregnancies, it's scary to even think about having sexual partners before you're ready to deal with the possible reactions that come along with it. What should alarm you the most is the fact that many people carrying the diseases don't even know that they have them. Some STD's can stay in your body for years without any signs of being infected.

The Human Immunodeficiency Virus (HIV) is an STD and is the virus that causes Acquired Immune Deficiency Syndrome (AIDS). It is found in the blood, semen and vaginal secretions of an infected person and is spread through unprotected sex, sharing needles and in very rare cases, through blood transfusions. HIV can hide out in the body for years without any symptoms so a person with the virus could spread the disease without even knowing it. A person with the virus compromises the body's ability to fight off infections. When the body can't fight off infections, the body deteriorates. Right now there is no cure for AIDS although there are some medical treatments that have been known to help with the symptoms.

Other common STD's such as chlamydia, genital herpes, and gonorrhea are lurking in the bodies of millions of people each day, some not realizing that they are infected and others that know but refuse to tell their partners. It's because of these instances that these diseases continue to spread worldwide.

The very best way to prevent any of these risks is through abstinence–not having sex at all, until you're ready to deal with the possibility of a pregnancy or diseases that will affect the rest of your life. If later you choose to be intimate with someone, be sure to use protection through birth control and other contraceptives used to fight pregnancy and disease. However, these methods of protection are not guaranteed.

When your body is used as a temple, you take full control of who you trust with it. It can only take one bad invitation to ruin the one temple that you've been given. Treat your temple with the utmost admiration by upholding its sacredness and by sharing it only with those deemed deserving of it.

What Goes On In the Temple Should Stay In the Temple

Temples have walls and doors for a reason. It keeps what's sacred protected by everything around it. These walls are usually of immaculate beauty decorated by statues, paintings and stained-glass windows. Yes, the beauty of any temple is always a sight to see! From the architecture to the artistry, those that work to upkeep its appearance take lots of time with the details.

When we're adorning our own temples, people can see from the outside just how meaningful our temples are. They may not all get the chance to see what it looks like on the inside, but you can judge a lot about a place from its exterior. This is why we have to be mindful of how we present our temples on the outside. Showing too much of what is sacred on the outside does two things; it exposes the outside elements to something very valuable and it attracts those that don't deserve the right to view it. Everything you wear as clothing should represent the goodness and purposeful person you are and nothing less. When you represent anything less than that (saggy pants or short, tight clothing, etc.) you misrepresent what's inside of the temple.

If nothing else, think of what you would wear into your place of worship. If it can't qualify as appropriate *in the temple*, does it qualify for others to see you in *as the temple* that you are?

If It's Not Holy Water, I Don't Need It

My parents' talk with me about substance abuse was really simple and in their own way. Mamma gave me a French cigarette one day and said, "Try this. I'd rather you do it around me than try to sneak a puff."

Just from being around her smoke, I knew it wasn't going to end up well. It didn't. I was sick the entire day and never touched a cigarette since then.

Daddy's method was less life threatening. One day while driving my brother and I back home he said to us, "You know, I promised to never do drugs when I was a young man and I never regretted that decision. Once you become an adult you can do what you please, but I suggest you make the right decision too…."

As he continued on, I zoned out at the thought that my daddy was actually once a young man. I don't know what he continued on about, but I got the picture. I've never regretted not doing drugs either. Mostly because it didn't seem that exciting to be zoned out more than I already tended to do when I was getting preached to, but most of all because Daddy had put the fear of God in me a long time ago. I don't remember him ever spanking me, but I know for a fact that he did. I probably passed out from it as he whipped the memory out of me.

Cheap Thrills: The Stinky Drug, the Silent Drug and the Social Drug

The addiction to smoking, drugs and alcohol are easy traps that many find themselves in because they come pretty cheap. But trust me, you get what you pay for. These are self-inflicted diseases are known to literally ruin peoples' lives.

Whenever you put anything into your body (your temple), it will naturally have a reaction to it. Because the body was made only to ingest food, other substances are foreign to the body so it reacts in order to protect itself. This is why there are side effects listed on medication bottles, but not on food labels.

An addiction is when a person continuously feeds their body with a substance to the point of dependency. Whenever a person is addicted to a substance, they will experience withdrawal symptoms such as sweating, nervousness or irritability. While there are certainly lots of types of addiction, let's take a look at the three major self afflicted addictions and how they affect your body. As we talk about them, imagine the feeling you'd have if you saw someone doing those things in your place of worship. Would you ever imagine smoking, doing drugs or drinking inside your place of sacredness? If not, why would you allow these same attacks to go on in your own temple?

Smoking-The Stinky Drug

Although smoking has been marketed to look glamorous, there's nothing glamorous about smoky breath, yellow teeth and dingy skin. Nor is there anything cute about lung cancer, throat cancer, asthma or emphysema. The nicotine in each cigarette keeps you coming back for more without you knowing which cigarette in the cute little box is going to be the one that kills you. It's like Russian rullet. Better yet, it's more like suicide. Cancer is the leading cause of death with tobacco being the most pinpointed factor.

Illegal and Prescription Drugs-The Silent Drug

I think of prescription drugs as a silent drug because most times, people take them when they're alone and sometimes their friends and family don't even know what's going on. Unfortunately, many people are found dead by the overdose of pills or from the body's reaction to the mixture of prescription drugs and other substances–usually alcohol. Taking any type of prescription that was not prescribed to you or that you use in excess for the purpose of feeling the side effects is harmful to your body, to your brain and is a test of luck.

Alcohol-The Social Drug

Just like cigarettes, alcohol is very much associated with social settings. Alcohol can be dressed up to look very enticing and although it's not illegal to drink, it's the over indulgence of alcohol that is destructive. Many people don't know when to stop drinking and the results of their actions are what's harmful. Not only does it affect the body (remember, anything that enters the body gets a reaction from the body), but it also affects the safety of you and others.

Alcohol is the fourth most addictive drug resulting in on average, ten to twelve less years of your life. Twenty-five percent of all suicides occur in alcoholics seventy-five percent of all murders involve alcohol use. Think you can handle your liquor? Think you can stop whenever you want? Don't fool yourself. Withdrawal from alcohol is said to be more severe than withdrawing from heroin and cocaine.

Fighting Against the Influence of Others

One of my main concerns and purpose of writing this section of the book comes from the large rate of biracial kids that decide to take part in these bad habits in efforts to deal with underlying issues. Studies show that young adults lacking a sense of self worth often run the risk of destructively tearing down their bodies through substance abuse. It's my hope that educating on the affects of these drugs will help you make wise decisions on your own actions.

But how do you say "no?" That's easy, just say it. Even a shake of the head gets the point across. You don't have to preach a sermon or hold a sign up to make your point. It has been my experience that if you look like you're comfortable in refusing to take part in something that you're not comfortable with, your peers will accept it and move on without trying to convince you otherwise. Besides, if you're maintaining a healthy temple, most times they will assume that you're not interested anyway. If nothing else, people respect a temple even if they don't believe in them. But if you're constantly being badgered by your friends to do those things to destroy your temple, then it's time you found some new friends! Contrary to popular belief, *not everyone* is doing it. However, if you have been put in a setting where you've decided to experiment with drugs and alcohol, it's never too late to quit.

Your temple is a place of sanctity and value. It's where your purpose is stored so that your actions can live them out. It's where your creator resides to live out that purpose. Once you take into account of all the wonderful value that you were born with, there's no room for anything less than what qualifies to enter the temple.

Just because I'm mixed doesn't mean I'm confused about the fact that my body is the only temple that I will ever receive. Given such gift, it is my duty to protect it from those things that are made to destroy it. I am committed to honoring my temple by having self control and qualifying what goes on around it and in it.

I've Discovered My Hairitage and I'm Not Afraid to Flaunt It

The most controversial part of being biracial is managing our hair. Our hair is the only physical feature that can be a mixture of more than one ethnic background. We may have our father's nose and our mother's lips, but there is never a combination of our father *and* mother's nose, or a mixture of *both* parent's lips. Because hair is the only physical feature that combines several ethnicities, it's often hard to find products that are made to suit us. Biracial hair has been a topic of discussion for a very long time and as the world of swirl continues to grow, so should our education on managing our hair.

Besides the unique characteristics of our hair that I believe every ethnicity carries, your hair is part of what makes you who you are. It's an important part of our day-to-day wardrobe. If it's not right, we walk out the door with less confidence than we could have had-if we walk out the door at all. This entire section is dedicated to understanding how hair works and the differences of hair types so that you can make the best purchasing and styling decisions. As always, there are lots of ongoing posts on my website and plenty of resources including a Hairitage consultation page. Above all, remember that your hair is also a part of your temple so the most important factor is that you keep it maintained and healthy. There's no such thing as "good hair" because all hair is good because it's just as unique as everything else about us.

It's been a learning process for me since the day my hair decided to start growing. As a baby, I didn't have much hair on my head, but when it started to grow, oh my what a sight! By the time I was five years old, if you wanted to brush my hair, you first had to put on your running shoes because you were in for a round of hide and seek! The very sound of a brush running through my hair was like nails on a chalkboard.

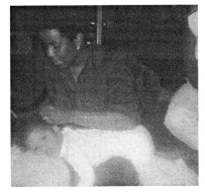

Before my first relaxer at age thirteen, my hair was very long, thick and wavy. Putting my hair in a ponytail consisted of lots of work to convince the hair to go in the same direction. Even with relaxed hair today, it takes at least three elastic bands to get my hair in a decent ponytail. Back in the day, my mother used actual rubber bands in my hair and they would snap against my ear as she wrestled my hair down. As anyone that knows me can tell you, I still have a fear of rubber bands to this day. Seriously.

Once I grew tired of playing by the creek with the boys and became more concerned about my appearance, I began locking myself up in the bathroom playing "scientist" as I mixed different lotions and creams together to find the best combination of products for my hair. I simply wanted hair that didn't frizz up by the time I got to school, and laid down when I wanted to play ball (Hey, I couldn't give up *everything* for the sake of beauty!). I wasn't sure what my overall style was, but all I knew is that for every hour my hair wasn't in a ponytail and braided down, it ensured me an hour of detangling the cotton candy cloud that covered my head afterwards. Most often, I thought I could feel the hair tangling up as my head also began to feel like it was heating up too.

I was certain that combing out my nest of hair was a form of child abuse. To ease the pain, my mom would let me try my hand at detangling my hair on my own first before she took a stab at it-which is exactly what it felt like. The angels were looking down on me the day someone showed my mother how to hold my hair tightly while brushing it. Before then, my head was lead by the brush. Whichever direction the brush went, is where my head fell. It wasn't until Mom began grabbing the section of hair and worked the brushing of my hair out from the ends to the scalp that I began thinking less and less that the brush was an evil object meant for punishment.

Once, my mom let me stay a whole week with some German friends of hers. With all day swimming every day, it was one of the best weeks of my life without a care in the world. Until it was time to go home.

When my mom came to pick me up, my hair was still in the two ponytails she had left me with, but they had shriveled up from being all the way down my back, to only shoulder length. I had not touched my hair the whole week-that's another reason why it was one of the best weeks of my life!

My mom and dad thought they would have to cut all of my hair off. Hours later, after washing, crying, conditioning, pleading, applying anti-tangling solutions (the whole

bottle), and a couple of fainting spells, my parents put me back together again. I'm sure that's the day that I became "tender headed."

To keep my hair moisturized on a regular basis, my mother used *Nivea* lotion on my natural hair, which worked fine, although she only used it because she didn't know what else to use. It worked on my dry legs so it proved its powers enough to be promoted to a hair product as well. Once I started using heat appliances to tame my hair's thickness, I was introduced to hair grease and pressing lotions which protected my hair from the heat, but also weighed my hair down. The heat appliances weren't made for course hair like mine so they didn't get hot enough to smooth the hair out completely, yet I was weighing it down with product to make up for it.

I knew that the day had come when I finally got it right when my mother said to me, "Oh I love your hair like that! It's not as greasy as it usually is!" She has a weird way of turning a compliment into an insult, but she meant well. I think. Germans tend to say *exactly* what's on their mind. Older German women tend to not care how it comes out.

After many trials and experimentations, I've learned that the best way to get my hair to behave is to maintain a head of healthy hair without fighting against its natural shape. I think everyone has to go through these sometimes extreme experiences to best understand what is best for their hair type. It's my hope that this section will help you to avoid some mistakes that many people make when they don't quite understand what their hair can and cannot do.

With so many different products on the market, it's often hard to distinguish what can actually work for us. Even the term "curly hair" products geared to multiethnic hair or natural styling, leave out some of us with textures between those lines. The problem is that most products are made either for mainstream consumers with products that can be very drying without providing us with enough moisture to keep the hair healthy, or ethnic products that can provide the moisture, but adds too much weight to the hair, making it hard to style without looking too greasy. (Yeah, Momma was right!)

To be sure that I give you the very best advice on managing your hair, I've brought in some of help from my own hair stylist and friend, Alisa "Barnsey" Barnes. With so much advice out there, I want to be sure that I'm not just speaking on my own experience of my own hair type, but that I'm giving you the best advice for all hair types. Each combination of nationality falls under these descriptions so I didn't leave anyone out.

If These Strands Could Talk

Hair care should be your first priority. No matter how much product you pile on, if your hair isn't healthy it *will not* give a healthy shine, lay straight, or curl correctly. Period. Lasting shine and healthy patterns only come from hair cuticles that aren't frayed or malnourished. Smooth and nourished hair cuticles only come from a healthy diet and the proper care of your specific type of hair.

Hair is made of a protein called *keratin*, which is also found in your skin and nails. Your hair is rooted into your scalp, feeding off the nutrients from the blood stream and the oil glands. A healthy diet keeps the body full of the nutrients which in turn, feeds to each and every keratin-filled strand of hair.

If your strands could talk, what would they say about how they've been fed lately? If they wouldn't have many nice things to say, it's most likely the reason why they're ignoring your attempts to get it to do what you want it to do.

A hair strand consists of the root, underneath the skin's surface and lives in the follicle which through genetics, determines your hair type. The shape of your follicle is one of the determining factors of your hair's shape. Straight or wavy hair stems from straight or somewhat slanted follicles. To give you a visual, imagine digging a hole in the ground in order to plant a tree. In order for the tree to stand up straight, you would dig the hole vertically as straight down into the ground as possible. That's an example of what follicles look like for straight hair. If you were to dig the hole, slanting to the left or right under the ground it would cause the tree to slant slightly, an example of a hair follicle for wavy hair. Curlier hair produces a flatter hair strand by the hair follicle having at a sharper and curvier angle underground, almost like a hook. Because of this, it comes out more like a curly ribbon. This is all determined genetically.

Once out of the follicle, the hair extends above the skin's surface. The hair that's visible to you is called the hair shaft which consists of three layers sitting on top of each other called the *medulla, cortex* and *cuticle.*

> *Medulla:* The innermost layer of the hair shaft is called the medulla, which is made of round cells. Because of curlier hair types' more flattened, ribbon-like shape of the hair strand, most curly hair doesn't contain a medulla. Still, those with straighter hair that do contain them, the medulla often doesn't run all the way down to the end of the hair shaft.

> *Cortex:* The next sleeve is called the cortex and is actually the thickest part of the hair strand. The cortex holds a lot of the characteristics of the hair such as its color, strength, moisture and resilience. I like to think of it as the brain of the hair strand because it's protected by the outer layer, yet controls most of the characteristics.

> *Cuticle:* The outermost sleeve (or the skin) that you actually see when you look at your hair is the cuticle, which is made by protein enriched keratin cells that overlap each other like fish scales. These fish scale-like cells have around seven to ten layers before you even get to the cortex. The number of layers determines the diameter of the hair. The more layers of cuticle your strands have, the thicker the hair.

The cuticle is believed to be the key component on determining the health of your hair. The smoother the cuticles lay, the smoother the surface. A smooth surface reflects light giving shine and allows the necessary oils from the skin's oil glands to travel all the way down to the ends of the hair. This is why straight haired people must wash their hair more often than those with a texture of more bend. Hair with more bend doesn't allow oils to travel as far down the hair strand as easily. This will become really important when we start talking about the types of products to use.

When your hair is damaged, the cuticles' scales have been broken or lifted from the hair shaft. Pulling the cuticles from their source of moisture and nutrients causes it to die off, exposing the cortex (the brain). Once exposed, the hair is permanently damaged and vulnerable to breakage. For those with hair that bends, extra efforts have to be made to keep the cuticles moisturized so the dryness doesn't cause breakage.

However your hair bends, it's important to know how to care for it accordingly. Regular wear and tear of your locks is a part of growing it, but in order for it to look its best you have to protect it from harm. Of course, your intentions when you brush your hair and use heated appliances aren't to destroy it, but it definitely happens when you do it in excess. Tie that in with an unhealthy diet and you don't give your hair a fighting chance! Meanwhile, we all make the mistake of buying any bottle of product that promises to encourage hair growth, strength and shine. Oh yes, if our hair strands could talk, they might sound a lot like my mother!

Coming from an African-American background, I've learned that many stylists in the Black salons will emphasize the need for moisture on my hair. This comes from the knowledge that ethnic textures are tighter than most other cultures. When the curls are tighter, it's harder for the natural oils to extend over to the ends of the hair strands, making the hair dry and fragile. To combat this issue, hair grease and pomades have been used to lock in moisture. In my experience, the overuse of product weighed my hair down and caused acne to my face and back from constant contact of hair products to my skin.

To combat these issues, I've gone to mainstream salons who underestimate my hair's need for moisture. After using a harsh shampoo to wash away the oil, they neglected to put any moisture back into my hair besides using some fancy conditioner – which was then washed out with water, leaving the strands stripped of the needed natural oils. To make up for the frizziness, they (freaked out) and tried to make up for it by adding a lot of heat to make the hair flat and straight. Now my hair was *dried* out and *fried* out.

To avoid such tragedies as these, be sure that the products that you're buying aren't simply building up on your hair which is sure to weigh it down. On the opposite end of the spectrum, check the ingredients to ensure that you're not putting on any products that contain anything that will dry it out. This must be a caution for every step along the way, from shampoos to styling products.

The key to healthy hair is hair that is well conditioned. So here comes your reality check. It's time to do a self assessment of exactly where your shine is actually coming from. Is it from the products you're using or the actual hair itself? Hair that's shiny but weighed down from product build up isn't the same as hair that's healthy and gives off a healthy shine.

If you've been mistaking your coated hair for conditioned hair, go through your products and start reading labels. Read on for my suggestions on what to look for in each type of product. We'll also talk more about the regular conditioning of your hair in a minute so that you can transform over from greasy hair to naturally shiny hair.

Determining Your Hair Type

Let's now talk about *your* particular hair type so that you can properly care for your own hair. This is where it gets tricky because like our skin color, there are so many ranges of hair types. Unlike a simple shade of skin color, your hair consists of three different dimensions that make up your hair type. Those dimensions include the *shape*, *volume* and *strength* of your hair.

To add to the confusion, just like our heritage, you can also have a combination of textures in different parts of your head. For example, my hair *shape* on my left side is a looser "S" shape than the right side. The most *voluminous* area with the most hair follicles per square inch is close to my crown *and* the hair *strength* is coarser in the back of my head than the front. Yeah, I'm definitely mixed! To top things off, even the first factor, the hair shape, is a mixture between wavy and curly. My hair is naturally wavy; however the ends tend to have a coily-curly shape. Talk about being of multi-hairitage!

If I confused you with those terms, let's break them all down to see how your hair is constructed. With five different shapes, three volume types and three strength ranges, there are over forty-five different combinations of hair types to fall under. Even if you have various differing sections like me, you should be able to come to an overall conclusion on where your hair lies in each category.

Shape

You hair's shape refers to how each individual hair naturally bends and twists creating coils, curls, kinks or waves. To most accurately determine your natural hair shape, examine your hair after shampooing and conditioning your hair, then letting it air dry naturally. Check one of the following shapes that describes your hair most accurately.

What shape most resembles the bend (if any) of your hair? Does it curl up like a spring, into an "O" or does it have an "O" shape, but it looks more like a corkscrew? Does your hair have a zigzag pattern like a "Z" or does it bend more like an "S?" Does it grow straight with no bend at all? What category does your hair fall into? Could it be a combination of shapes?

Shape	Description
Coily-Kinky	Locks of hair are curled very tightly into an "O" shape with a diameter of 1/8" to 1/4" like a spring
Coily-Curly	Locks of hair that have a defined "O" shaped looped into a corkscrew affect with curly diameter approximately 3/8" and larger
Kinky	Locks of hair having a zigzag "Z" pattern without ever creating the "O" of coily hair. The bends are very small and frequent.
Wavy	Locks of hair with a loose "S" shape without ever creating the shape of an "O." The bends tend to be infrequent, only occurring about every 1 inch or greater
Straight	Locks of hair with no bend at all

Volume

Volume refers to the number of hair strands per square inch. Often times, people confuse volume with hair that has a thick diameter. In this case however, it's actually determined by parting the hair and examining the number of strands extending out of the scalp.

Part your hair and notice how dense your hair is, by looking at the amount of hair follicles sprouting hair. How exposed is your scalp visually? The less visually exposed your scalp is, the denser your volume. Check which one of the following that best describes your scalp.

Volume	Description
Very Dense	Very dense amount of hair, when you cannot see the scalp without parting the hair, nor can you see through the strands of hair.
Mildly Dense	Mildly dense amount of hair where you can see through very few sections of hair.
Fine	Lower number of hair on the head and you may be able to see the scalp when hair moves

Strength

Strength refers to the diameter of each individual hair strand and is determined by the number of cuticle layers on the hair shaft. Knowing your hair's texture saves you from using too much heat when styling so that you don't burn through the cuticles.

With so many variations, one can end up with any combination of the three characteristics. Even siblings with the same parents can have different hair types. After deciding on what combination of hair terms you have, read on to learn about the different products on the market. There's also a guide on the Swirl Power site to give you specific advice on your hair type so you can determine what types of products are best for you.

Strength	Description
Course	Hair strands are thick and strong
Medium	Hair strands are of medium thickness and fairly strong
Thin	Hair strands are thin and fragile

Finding the Right Products

Cleansing, conditioning and styling are the three components of basic hair care. As simple as it may seem, it gets overwhelming when you step into the aisles of hair products. Basic hair care products include a shampoo, conditioner, styling products and styling tools. Before we begin discussing certain types of products, remember that hair products were invented centuries after hair was first created. Shampoos, conditioners or any other hair product aren't bare essentials for surviving so don't be a slave to the thought that you *have to have* the most expensive brand of products in order to get the best results. Don't spend so much time deciding on products based on packaging. Instead, invest the time in reading ingredient labels. *The care of your hair determines its appearance, not the product.* Read this entire chapter before your next visit down the beauty aisle to save yourself from going broke based on an empty promise.

Shampoos

Shampoos are made to cleanse the scalp and hair with the focus mainly on the scalp. Cleansing the scalp unclogs pores and stimulates the flow of blood to the scalp. In doing so, you dislodge the dirt and residue without stripping away the oil or *sebum*, from the hair follicle. This is done by massaging the scalp with the pads of your fingers.

While shampooing textured hair, focus mainly on the scalp as the product will do most of the needed work on the rest of the hair when you're rinsing it out. Shampoos are made to clean the scalp and conditioners are made for the hair. Working in too much product on the rest of the hair will dry it out of the needed oils. Also, never pile your hair on top of your head when washing. Those shampoo commercials on television aren't with our hair in mind. Straighter hair types with little to no bend should work up a good lather on the hair to rid it of product build up, but be very mindful of not stripping it of all the needed oils.

For those of you that have used a lot of wax based products in the past to coat your hair in the name of conditioning, you may also have to use a little bit of shampoo on the strands in order to shampoo the product out. Start off with using a clarifying shampoo to remove all unwanted products from the hair and follow up with a moisturizing shampoo to infuse moisture back into the hair.

For biracial textured hair the "squeaky clean" approach isn't the way to go when determining whether or not your hair is clean. This often means that the hair strands no longer have any oils on the cuticle which could spell dry hair and frizziness if you don't properly condition immediately afterwards.

The number of times per week to wash your hair depends solely on the amount of oil that your scalp produces and how far down it travels down the shaft. If your hair ranges between straight to wavy, the natural oils will travel down to the hair's end faster and you may want to wash it a couple of times throughout the week. Kinky to coily hair can go a week or so without washing in order to keep the oils traveling down to the ends. Because of the twist and turns of the hair, these oils don't travel down the strands as easily. If however, you don't want to rob your scalp of its oils, but it feels a little heavier than it should, a simple rinse of warm to hot water while massaging the scalp works just as well.

Finding the Right Shampoo for You

When looking for shampoos, look for products that are *alcohol-free.* You may also see products that are "paraben-free," meaning that they don't contain preservatives that have been known to mimic small portions of estrogen linked to breast cancer although it's not a proven fact. However, the rule of thumb is that the less man-made chemicals, the better. Some of the better ingredients for your hair include:

➢ Ammonium lauryl sulfate

➢ Cocamidoprpyl betaine,

➢ Lauramide DEA

➢ Propylene glycol

➢ Sodium laureth sulfate

These ingredients should at least be listed within the first five ingredients to qualify as actually being an active ingredient. Look past the fruit flavor scents and silicone based products when selecting a shampoo. These factors are all irrelevant at this stage of the game. The great smelling shampoos will be washed out by the conditioner and silicone isn't necessary until *after* the cleansing step. The main focus is on the cleansing of the scalp without over drying or leaving a residue on the hair.

Since shampoos work much like soap, you don't have to invest all of your money in expensive products because they mostly do the same job although some are better than other. You get what you pay for, but you should not have to pay an arm and a leg. However, I say that with the caution of using products with the following ingredients.

These ingredients are known to be very harsh to most hair types by causing dryness and skin irritation:

> - Akyl sodium sulfate

> - Alkyl benzene sulfonate

> - Ammonium xylensesulfate

> - Sodim coco-sulfate

> - Sodium C-14-16

> - Sodium dodecylbenzenesulfonate

> - Sodium lauryl Sulfate (Similar to laureth, but does just the opposite)

> - TEA-dodecylbenzene

> - TEA-dodecylebenzesulfonate

> - TEA-laurylsufate

Besides the ingredients, there are also some terms on the front label that you will also want to pay attention to. Always define your shampoo as a clarifying (or a daily) shampoo or moisturizing (also called a conditioning) shampoo. Here's the difference:

Clarifying Shampoos

Clarifying shampoos function as super cleansers. These are most times the cheaper brands on the shelves because it's the standard type of shampoo made. Most hotel shampoos are clarifying shampoos. They remove unwanted detergents, giving your hair a fresh start and restores natural shine. Those with strands that can stand the potency such as the wavy and straight hair shapes, are encouraged to use these as needed. If your hair is naturally dry, I don't recommend regular use of clarifying shampoos unless using them every now and then to fight the buildup of styling products. In these cases, be sure that you make up for the harshness by following up with a moisturizing shampoo to replenish the ph balance.

Moisturizing Shampoos

Moisturizing shampoos balance the ph of the hair at its natural level by rehydrating it. Those with kinky, coily and curly shapes should go with a product that is creamy (most clarifying shampoos are foamy) and is made for "dry" or "chemically treated hair" even if your hair isn't chemically treated. I've found the thicker products to be those targeted for African American hair. If you find that a moisturizing shampoo is too heavy, try using a clarifying shampoo lightly during the first cleansing and following up with a moisturizing shampoo the second time around. You can also mix the two together in your hands before applying to the hair.

Conditioners

Moisturizing the hair after the scalp is clean by conditioning is the next step. Replenishing moisture is the primary goal of conditioners. This step is my favorite part of the process because it helps to detangle while capturing the hair at its most moisturized and flexible state. With any type of textured hair you should never be easy on the conditioner. Saturate the hair with conditioner by applying the conditioner evenly throughout the hair. Those with long hair should apply conditioner from ends to roots.

Those with fine hair can rinse out shortly afterwards while others should wait about five to fifteen minutes before rinsing. While waiting, you can use a plastic cap to cover the head in order to keep the body's heat confined, which helps the conditioner penetrate the strands. You can also sit under a hooded dryer for up to fifteen minutes in order for the heat to help with the penetration. Finer hair requires less conditioning which would weigh the hair down.

When rinsing, begin detangling with your fingers or a wide tooth comb. Rinsing your hair is a critical step in the conditioning process because you have to use your sense of touch to decide whether or not you've rinsed enough of the conditioner out of your hair. If after rinsing, your hair feels squeaky, you've rinsed too much of the conditioner out. Reapply more conditioner and rinse again before moving on. Everyone's hair is different and after a few times, you'll get the hang of what feels right. Also, if you plan on wearing your hair in its natural state by letting it air dry, you may want to leave a little bit of the conditioner in the hair even if you plan on following up with a leave-in conditioner.

Once the tangles are gone and it's time to rinse out, the hair is at its softest point. Towel dry by squeezing most of the water from your hair, but never running the towel back and forth across the hair. This causes frizz and damage to the hair cuticles.

Finding the Right Conditioner for You

When you're checking your product labels, look for true moisturizing ingredients such as:

➢ Castor oil

➢ Cholesterol

➢ Lanolin

➢ Shea butter

➢ Coconut Oil

These natural oils provide moisture and protection over the strands. Again, fruity smelling products that don't contain any of these ingredients aren't worth spending your extra dollars on with the hopes of giving your hair a real conditioning experience.

The type of conditioner you use depends on the hair texture and whether or not you've chemically altered your hair. Most guys don't alter their hair using chemicals and should simply look at how much weight the product puts on their hair. Keep in mind that straight and wavy shapes have a smoother cuticle surface while the kinky, coily and curlies have a raised cuticle surface. Because of this, the richness of the conditioner needed will depend on your hair shape. The creamier the conditioner, the more appropriate it is for tighter, coily hair shapes.

Be mindful of products being marketed as having natural ingredients as many manufacturers stick pictures of trees and exotic fruits to entice you. Know what's naturally made and what products simply have natural fragrances as ingredients. For example, look for a listing of coconut oil, not coconut fragrance in the ingredient listing.

If your scalp requires some extra condition to soothe the scalp, try some of these natural essential oils that provide the moisture:

➤ Almond

➤ Coconut Oil

➤ Castor Seed Oil

➤ Eucalyptus

➤ Jojoba

➤ Olive Oil

➤ Tea tree

On the contrary, look out for these ingredients that tend to dry out the hair. When trying to spot out these ingredients, look for them in the beginning of the ingredient label. The top five ingredients listed actually make up the product while anything listed beyond the fragrance only comes in small doses and are barely affective.

➤ Ethanol

➤ Ethyl Alcohol

➤ Ingredients with Copolyol, Acrylate, Vinyl or PVP in the name

➤ Isopropyl Alcohol

➤ Potassium Chloride

- ➢ SD Alcohol 40

- ➢ Sodium Bicarbonate (baking soda)

- ➢ Sodium Chloride

When wearing your hair in its natural texture, look for conditioning products that have a weight, slip and emollient ingredient. Weight ingredients allow the curls, kinks and waves to clump together and hang down (instead of in the air). Some favorites of Teri LaFlesh, author of *Curly Like Me* are *stearyl alcohol, cetyl alcohol and cetearyl alcohol.* Even though I'm not necessarily a curly, I agree with her. These ingredients are light, but allow the hair to form its natural shape. Slip ingredients allow combing through the hair to be an easier task. Some of these ingredients include silicones like *dimethecone* and *cyclomethicone* or the ingredient *stearamidopropyl dimethylamine.* Moisturizing ingredients such as the essential oils listed earlier make up the emollient ingredients. These are natural ingredients that are known to penetrate the hair shaft.

Cream Rinses

Cream rinses are designed to soften hair, add luster and detangle. They're usually for those with very fine hair with a thin diameter per strand. These are the mini bottles available in hotels even when they use words like "conditioning" on the label. Because the other conditioners may be too heavy, the cream rinses make the hair manageable to comb without the weight. When using them, be careful not to use too frequently to avoid buildup.

Protein Conditioners

Anyone with chemically treated hair should use a protein conditioner containing the protein keratin which replenishes the protein lost in the chemical process. It works by passing through the cuticle layers to get to the cortex. Strengthening the cortex intensifies the hair and increasing the elasticity. However, you *can* overdo it so be careful and don't use protein conditioners too often. Doing so can be drying and will defeat the purpose. To avoid this, rotate with a regular moisturizing conditioner.

Leave-In Conditioners

The mineral oil in leave-in conditioners are used to keep the hair soft and differs in the regular conditioners because (as the name implies), you leave the product in the hair after the hair is conditioned. Some product lines use the leave-in conditioners as a product that allows the hair to lock into its natural pattern by using moisturizing ingredients of a conditioner. Most guys or ladies with short styles can use leave-in conditioners instead of hair gel (which often can be drying) to lock the curls, kinks or coils together.

The amount of product to use depends on the volume and strength of your hair. Start off using a dime-size for your entire head and distributing it evenly by applying in sections of the hair. Add more product if needed. If your hair becomes too stiff or hard once it starts to dry, ease up on the amount. If you're wearing your hair in its natural state, you can add more product after the hair is dry in order to help lock the sections together while adding moisture. If you plan on using heat on your hair afterwards, use just enough to protect the hair from the upcoming heat wave so that you don't harm the cuticles, but not too much that it weighs the hair down.

Deep Conditioners

Deep conditioners are imperative for hair that craves moisture. These products are the creamiest conditioning products available. After applying to the hair (emphasizing a lot of product on the ends), let it sit on the hair for three to five minutes with a towel over your head or by covering your hair with a plastic cap and sitting under a hooded dryer for fifteen minutes. The hooded dryer approach is optimal for deep conditioning because the heat helps the conditioner penetrate the hair shaft. Weekly deep conditioning has been the key to those with long lengths and dense volumes by keeping the hair moisturized throughout the entire hair strand.

Styling Products

Styling products are used to help (you guessed it) style the hair. Whether your hair is worn natural or has been chemically treated, your hair is affected by any product applied to it. To get the best distribution of product on to the hair, place a dab into your palm and rub your palms together to emulsify the product before applying. The following products are the main products that are sold.

Gels, Mousses and Sprays

Although I'm not a fan of gels, mousses or hair sprays because of their drying affects, there are some products that combat those issues. An example of these is conditioning gels. These work best on wavy and straight shapes with a fine texture that have smooth enough cuticle patterns to stand the possible dryness from the alcohol ingredients. If you're looking for a product to keep your curls and other textures together, any type of foaming mousse, gel or hair spray aren't necessarily the best way. Look to conditioners to lock textures together instead of these products.

Pomades

Pomades are wax-based products typically used to control stray hairs and to add volume to short styles. If you've confessed to coating instead of conditioning your hair and you have been using pomades, this will be the reason for the product buildup. Pomades are usually really thick, containing a petroleum jelly-based substance and is very hard to remove from the hair. The best way to remove the build up is by using a clarifying shampoo. If you're looking to grow your hair out to a longer length, pomades should be left alone as the thick substance also clogs the scalp, preventing the hair follicles from breathing.

Setting and Sculpting Lotions

Setting lotions provide shine to the hair and adhere to all hair types by helping the hair set once it's dry. These are used most times when roller setting the hair. This is where a lot of African-American stylists go wrong with biracial hair. They tend to use too much of the product, making the hair hard and sticky once it's dry.

The lotions come in both foam and liquid versions. If using the foam, be sure that your hair has enough water still in it to balance out the amount of foam used. If using the liquid version, I suggest balancing it out in a squirt bottle with about 2/3 water. In both cases, keeping the hair saturated with water keeps the hair flexible to roll onto rollers and prevents you from using too much product on the hair.

Sculpting lotions work somewhat like the setting lotions although they're typically used for wavy and straight hair. These lotions are great when you want a slightly crisp hold without using any heating tools.

Silicone Serums

Silicone serums add shine to the hair while controlling the frizz. These serums are a water-soluble liquid with an oily feel to the touch. However, once applied to the hair, there isn't an oily feel to them because silicone serums are actually made from a plastic called *dimethicone*. Because too much silicone can dry the hair out, all serums should be evenly distributed in the hair when the hair is wet. It works by smoothing out the cuticle either for fighting humidity or heat when using a styling tool. If used on dry hair before styling, avoid adding too many layers of it which will dry out the cuticles over time. I must warn you: *There is no serum that will completely free you from frizz which is simply a characteristic of textured hair.*

Expect to see other ingredients that help make the hair slippery to comb through, although they evaporate once the hair dries so they don't stick around to help fight the frizz. Two ingredients that are known to do so are *cyclomethicone* and *cyclopentasiloxane*.

Relaxing the Hair vs. Going Natural

Relaxing the hair involves using a chemical to straighten out the shape of the hair's natural state. This is often used by women of color with tight hair shapes. For some, not only does relaxing help to release the tightness of the hair's shape, but it also helps with frizz. The one thing to remember about the relaxer is that is *not* reversible. Once you relax the hair, the only way to go back to being natural is to grow it out. A relaxer is simply a milder version of the perm while the texturizer is a milder version of the relaxer. In marketing terms, perms, no-lye relaxers, thermal straighteners, or texturizers all carry the same purpose. Same game, different name. The chemical strengths just vary.

Another factor to consider is that hair relaxing treatments consist of a chemical and you risk hair breakage and scalp reactions to those chemicals, especially if they're applied often. *When coloring or relaxing the hair, it loses at least ten percent of its strength.* Thermal straighteners work a little differently by adding on to the strand, but they wash out over time.

I'm often asked how young is *too* young to start relaxing a girl's hair. I personally don't suggest relaxers for girls under the age of thirteen simply because I think young girls should appreciate the natural beauty they possess, especially if their hair seems to be different from their peers. What makes us different also makes us unique. How can we appreciate who we are if we're already changing part of what makes us so distinctive? Not only that, but the maintenance of a relaxer must be kept up to avoid hair breakage over time and this requires the responsibility of a young woman who can handle it.

Most of my friends (including myself) have gone back to wearing their hair natural after years of relaxing. Some of us see it as a way of coming into our own self acceptance while others are trying to repair the damage of the chemical processing. I see it as both. After the chemical has been applied over the years, the hair becomes very fragile and if you add coloring on top of it, the hair becomes very dry with little to no elasticity over time. Embracing your natural hair is a direct expression of pride in who you are and has become increasingly popular. As long as you keep your hair healthy, it's regarded as one of the most unique features of multiracial people. While natural hair tends to grow faster, it may also mean more day-to-day maintenance and styling unless the hair is worn in twists or dreads. Just like chemically treated hair, natural hair must be conditioned on a regular basis to maintain a healthy shine and flexibility.

Whether you go natural or use a chemical to color or relax the hair, keeping the scalp clean and the hair strands nourished are top priority. While coily and kinky shapes or hair that's been chemically treated hair requires more efforts to do so, all methods should focus on both of these issues. Although hair breakage is normal, excessive shedding should be looked at closely as it may mean a problem with your diet or your styling regimen. This is a direct signal that your hair is thirsty and needs moisture to restore its natural oils. This is true for all shapes, including those with no bend. Your strands are talking so listen up as they may be whispering while on their death bed.

Don't Believe the Hype

Most of us have gone through the trial and error periods of finding what works for our hair. Many of you are reading this section as part of your learning process because of your desperate need to find the answer to your hair issues. And let's be honest with ourselves, we've made hair product companies a whole lot of money based on our desperation! In this section, I'll touch base on some of the recent products that leave us unfulfilled customers still looking for a cure.

Texture Promises

Do not be fooled by products promising to make your hair curly or straightening balms to straighten out your hair. These products are only to *enhance* what's already there so if you have naturally curly hair the product will at best, help define your curls. It will not however, magically make your naturally straight hair curly. Your hair can't be tricked into doing something that it's genetically not built for. Remember, the hair follicle *underneath* the scalp determines the texture of your hair, not a product.

Your Fight Against Frizz and Humidity

The fight against frizz and humidity is something that a Southern girl like me knows all about –especially when rocking a natural head of hair with no chemicals to relax the curl. Because textured hair is naturally dry with raised cuticles, humidity is attracted to it and latches on to the dry surface of your hair shaft. It fills into those pockets of the hair shaft and because our hair naturally bends in different directions, you've got each strand going in whatever direction it wants to go in.

To combat the frizzies, shampoo less and condition more in order to fill in the cracked areas that cause the hair to frizz. This is especially true for the ends of the hair that becomes frayed from heat appliances and natural wear and tear. The less room for humidity to latch on to, the less frizz you'll have. At the end of the day, frizz is a characteristic of having a head full of textured hair. There is no magic product to erase the entire frizz all together, but there are some tricks to minimize it.

Faster Hair Growth Through Trimming or Products

Despite this long lived theory, cutting the dead ends won't make your hair grow faster nor will any product that you apply to it. Remember, your hair grows from the scalp, not the ends of your hair. Trimming the ends will, at best, allow your hair to continue growing without damaged split ends growing up the hair shaft. If you're looking to grow your hair longer, only trim your hair if you see that your ends are damaged. If there isn't any damage, there's no need to cutting off what's not dead.

Shampooing the scalp and conditioning the hair along with the proper styling techniques are sure ways to stay on track for caring for the hair. Since the hair grows from the scalp, the scalp must be cleaned of any dirt and oil (which is why greasing the scalp doesn't really work). Any help with growth should be focused on the scalp area only. Think of it just as you would fertilize a plant, you would add fertilizer to the soil, not the leaves, right? Same goes for your hair. Take care of the scalp (the soil) to keep it growing. Trim off any damaged ends (the leaves) so that the decay doesn't spread throughout. Continue constant maintenance of what has grown by caring for it regularly.

Expensive Brands and Fancy Packaging

In recent years a lot of product manufacturers have created the idea that the more expensive brands of shampoo and conditioners work to make your hair somehow cleaner and healthier than the less expensive ones. This however isn't always the case. The bigger question instead should be what type of ingredients are you investing in?

These "nutrient enriched" creams are said to be "infused" with nutrients that if they *are* infused in anyway, the infused ingredients are too large to even be absorbed by the hair. Again, the ingredient labels tell it all. Look past the promises in the front of the bottle and read the product facts in the label. Also, be cautious of conditioners that state the promise to "repair" the damaged hair. Since hair is made up of the same protein as nails, this would be like promising to repair a broken nail. It's just impossible. Damaged hair has already lost the fight and it's too late to recover it. The best thing to do is to cut the damaged hair off.

Multitasking Products

Ever wonder how the products labeled as "Hair and Body Cleansers" were able to make it on to store shelves? Well essentially, they qualify to do the same job since your scalp is technically your skin –just with a lot of hair on it. I'm not convinced yet that this is the best route to go, but if you have really short hair and are out of shampoo, it can't hurt. Just be sure to follow up with a good conditioner.

Another multitasking product is the 2-in-1 shampoos and conditioners. While the concept sounds great, there are some things that just are better off separated. Trying to simplify the (already simple) process leaves room for you to be cheated out of the benefits. The product is either cheating you on the cleansing or it's not moisturizing. Most likely, it contains silicone which doesn't wash off with water when rinsing. This would be the "conditioning" part of a 2-in-1 shampoo and conditioner. I think we can both agree that your hair deserves more treatment than that. Take the time to do both steps separately, cleansing the scalp and conditioning the hair. When purchasing products, buy shampoos according to the needs of your scalp. Purchase conditioners according to the needs of your hair. These separate products may or may not be from the same hair care line.

Another multi-tasking product is the color and relaxer systems that allow you to color and relax the hair at the same time. This, in theory, cuts down on the weeks required for waiting between each process. Although it may seem like a good idea, neither of these chemical processes is encouraged to be tried outside of a licensed stylist.

Adding chemical to the hair is already a risk and adding two types of chemicals is a double risk.

Product Junkies Anonymous

With the insider information given, it's time to start reading labels and spring cleaning those shelves full of half-used products. Look over the ingredients I mentioned earlier to narrow down the products that can stay and those that should be tossed. If you still can't part with some of your products, here are some ideas of alternative uses for the products that don't make the final cut.

➢ Transform shampoos that don't make the cut into cleansers for your makeup brushes and hair brushes. Wet the brushes before applying the shampoo onto them and working them into a later. Rinse and let dry.

➢ Pour unwanted shampoo into a hand-soap pump to use as a hand washing soap.

➢ Stuck with watery conditioners that slip right through your hair? Using unproductive conditioners as a shaving cream is an alternative use. Simply apply to the skin as you would using having cream and shave off with a razor.

➢ 2-in1 shampoos and conditioners don't have to go to waste. Use them as a moisturizing shampoo, but still apply conditioner afterwards.

➢ Combining a watery conditioner with a thicker form such as a hair masque makes the masque easier to apply to the hair. Add a dab or two into the masque cream and rub together before applying to the hair.

➢ Hair moisturizing creams that are moisturizing, but make the hair really greasy can be used as spot treatments. Apply only to the ends on the days when you're styling your hair, but plan on washing the next day. Some creams can be applied to the entire head the night before you wash the hair to give it a boost of moisture before shampooing.

➢ Styling products that you now know aren't made for your hair type don't have to go to waste. Talk to friends that have different textures than you and may be able to use them.

Hair Maintenance and Recommendations

Consistency is key when it comes to the maintenance of your hair no matter the type and this goes for both men and women. While the product brands may change, the efforts should not. Go to the website *www.SwirlPower.com* for the latest recommendations; most are available to order online through the online store.

Here are my final rules on how to maintain your hair on a consistent basis to ensure a head full of healthy hair that will definitely make you ready for the "spot" light.

Swim-Proof Hair

A major concern for long and/or chemically-treated hair is the time it takes to care for hair after swimming. Salt water and chlorine can be corrosive to the hair while the water tangles it up.

To combat the hair damage, coat the hair lightly with a natural oil or silicone before taking a dip, as these oils don't rinse off easily. Braid the hair down in one or more braids to keep the hair from tangling in the water and secure them tightly. Once swim time is over, unravel the hair and shampoo as usual then follow up with lots of conditioner.

Combing and Brushing

Be sure to comb or brush the hair by working from the ends to the roots. In between the scalp and those areas being brushed, grab hold of the hair and squeeze tightly to block the tension of detangling from your scalp which causes the pain. If necessary, section the hair off in parts to take the hair on as four small challenges. Also look for brushes with rubber or natural bristles.

When looking for combs and brushes for textured hair look for combs that are wide toothed and brushes with straight bristles, preferably without the balls on the top of them. These bristles tend to snag the hair easier.

Coily-Kinky Hair Types

Shampoo: Moisturizing or Conditioning Shampoo

Conditioner: Deep Conditioner

Products: Setting Lotion, Leave-In Conditioner, Silicone Serum, Moisturizing Lotion, Natural Oils, Pomade (for light styling only)

Description:

Coily-kinky hair has lots of flexibility and strength to hold different styles. The hair locks are curled very tightly into an "O" shape like a spring. These looped patterns have cuticle layers that are typically raised up. This hair shape doesn't allow the oils to reach the end of the strands as easily so the hair naturally lacks a lot of shine. Because of this, it is extremely fragile despite the appearance of volume. Make no mistake though, just because the hair has a tighter shape doesn't mean that it's also course. Most textures such as these are very fragile and thin. In order to straighten this type, you must flatten the cuticle with heat. While courser hair can withstand more heat, the lesser strengths should keep the heat temperatures to a safer level. Short styles may experience razor bumps and ingrown hairs because of the natural curl of the hair.

Recommendations:

• Even if your hair isn't chemically treated for straightening or coloring, look for products that cater to these issues. These products hold the richer forms and most moisturizing ingredients.

• Stay away from 2-in1's and dandruff shampoos which are too drying for your particular hair type.

• Look for conditioners that contain stearyl alcohol, cetyl alcohol, ceteary alcohol or glycerin as the first five ingredients listed. Natural oils such as coconut, olive and shea butter are also great for moisturizing and should be applied to the hair throughout the week.

• Deep conditioning is recommended after each shampooing.

• Only use pomades for light styling as they contain petroleum jelly substances which are hard to wash out.

Kinky Hair Types

Shampoo: Moisturizing or Conditioning Shampoo

Conditioner: Deep Conditioner

Products: Setting Lotion, Leave-In Conditioner, Moisturizing Lotion, Natural Oils, Pomade (for light styling only)

Description:

Kinky hair has a very intricate shape that allows it to hold styles that have lots of bend. This hair type is very manageable while wearing in its natural state and/or braided styles. Although it comes in a variety of shapes, the best way to describe kinky hair is hair that has a zigzag "Z" pattern without ever creating the "O" of coily hair. These textured patterns have cuticle layers that are typically raised up. The bends are very small and frequent which prevent oils from reaching the end of the strands so it is naturally fragile and lacks in shine. In order to straighten this type, you must flatten the cuticle with heat, preferably with a product that locks in moisture. While courser hair can withstand more heat, the lesser strengths should keep the heat temperatures to a safer level.

Recommendations:

• Even if your hair isn't chemically treated for straightening or coloring, look for products that cater to these issues. These products hold the richer forms and most moisturizing ingredients

• Stay away from 2-in1's and dandruff shampoos which are too drying for your particular hair type.

• Look for conditioners that contain stearyl alcohol, cetyl alcohol, ceteary alcohol or glycerin as the first five ingredients listed. Natural oils such as coconut, olive and shea butter are also great for moisturizing. Apply to the ends of the hair regularly to avoid damaged ends.

• Deep conditioning is recommended after each shampooing.

• Apply leave-in conditioners while the hair is wet and follow up other moisturizing products throughout the week.

• Only use pomades for light styling as they contain petroleum jelly substances which are hard to wash out.

Coily-Curly Hair Types

Shampoo: Moisturizing Shampoo

Conditioner: Deep Conditioner, Moisturizing Conditioner

Products: Setting Lotion, Leave-In Conditioner, Silicone Serum, Moisturizing Lotion (on courser textures), Natural Oils

Description:

      Coily-curly hair has a variety of fun curly textures with a defined "O" shaped looped into a corkscrew affect. These looped patterns have cuticle layers that are typically raised up. Naturally lacking in shine, the shape doesn't allow the oils to reach the end of the strands very easily. Because of this, thin to medium strengths are extremely fragile despite the appearance of volume. Most coily hair is thinner than straight hair although the texture makes us think otherwise. In order to straighten this type, you must flatten the cuticle with heat, preferably with a product that locks in moisture. While courser hair can withstand more heat, the lesser strengths should keep the heat temperatures to a safer level. Short styles may experience razor bumps and ingrown hairs because of the natural curl of the hair.

Recommendations:

• Even if your hair isn't chemically treated for straightening or coloring, look for products that cater to these issues. These products hold the richer forms and most moisturizing ingredients.

• If the shampoos or conditioners are weighing your hair down, switch to a less creamy product that is just as moisturizing, but isn't too watery.

• Stay away from 2-in1's and dandruff shampoos which are too drying for your particular hair type.

• Look for conditioners that contain stearyl alcohol, cetyl alcohol, ceteary alcohol or glycerin as the first five ingredients listed. Natural oils such as coconut, olive and shea butter are also great for moisturizing. Apply to the ends of the hair regularly to avoid damaged ends. Once ends are damaged, they can't be repaired.

• Deep conditioning is recommended although finer strengths can use moisturizing conditioners and deep conditioners instead.

Wavy Hair Types

Shampoo: Clarifying then Moisturizing Shampoo (alternate as needed)

Conditioner: Deep Conditioner, Moisturizing Conditioner, Cream Rinse

Products: Sculpting Lotion, Setting Lotion, Leave-In Conditioner, Silicone Serum, Sculpting Conditioning Gels, Moisturizing Lotion (lightly as needed on courser textures)

Description:

Wavy hair has the shine of straight hair and flexibility of more textured hair. It holds a loose "S" shape without ever creating the shape of an "O" with infrequent bends. The cuticles lie flat, giving off the look of shine. These wavy patterns can be very defined or loose. Care for this type borders between that of textured or straighter hair, depending on the frequency and strength of the strands. The weight of the product is also dependent on the strength and volume of the hair. The lesser the strength and volume, the less creamy the product is required. In order to straighten this type, you must flatten the cuticle with heat, preferably with a product that locks in moisture. Product distribution on the hair should be very light and even to avoid too much product in certain areas. While courser hair can withstand more heat, the lesser strengths should keep the heat temperatures to a safer level.

Recommendations:

• Alternating between clarifying and moisturizing shampoos keeps the ph balance in the hair without stripping it of the oils needed. After a few attempts, you will know whether or not you should alternate each week or during each shampoo process. Always switch to moisturizing if the hair is dry or to the clarifying shampoo if there's a lot of buildup.

• Stay away from 2-in1's and dandruff shampoos if they are too drying for your particular hair type and only list silicone as the conditioning ingredient.

• The thinner strengths are recommended to use moisturized conditioners or cream rinses, although if the hair still feels dry, upgrade to a creamier product: Cream rinses upgraded to a moisturizing conditioner, moisturizing conditioners upgraded to a deep conditioning product. These products contain a greater amount of stearyl alcohol, cetyl alcohol, ceteary alcohol or glycerin and should be listed within the first five ingredients on the label.

• Deep conditioning is recommended for courser hair with frequent wave patterns while less creamier conditioners are great for thinner strengths.

• While setting lotions are flexible for all hair types, sculpting lotions are lighter and allow the hair to keep the texture of loose wavy styles.

• Apply light leave-in conditioners and silicone serums while the hair is wet.

Straight Hair Types

Shampoo: Clarifying or Moisturizing Shampoo (alternate as needed)

Conditioner: Moisturizing Conditioner or Cream Rinse

Products: Sculpting Lotion, Sculpting Conditioning Gels, Mousse

Description:

      Straight hair types usually have a flat cuticle base giving it no bend at all. Straight hair holds lots of shine and usually don't require heat for straightening. Because the oils run down the strands easier than textured hair, it must be washed more frequently. Conditioning of the hair is still necessary although the weight of the product should remain pretty light. The lesser the strength and volume, the less creamy the product should be. The diameter of this texture can be quite small, giving it little strength and making it susceptible to breakage if handled harshly. To create temporary curls, use heated rollers on dry hair. Heat should be used based on the hair's ability to withstand the heat. While the hair is naturally straight, heat may also be used to smooth the cuticles down for a smoother finish.

Recommendations:

• Most straight hair has the ability to withstand clarifying shampoos and cream rinses. However, if the hair still feels dry, upgrade to a creamier product.

• Alternating between clarifying and moisturizing shampoos keeps the ph balance in the hair without stripping it of the oils needed. After a few attempts, you will know whether or not you should alternate each week or during each shampoo process. Always switch to moisturizing if the hair is dry or to the clarifying if there's a lot of buildup.

• "Daily shampoos" are another name for clarifying shampoos.

• Try conditioning gels before sculpting gets in order to avoid the alcohol levels which can be drying to any hair type.

    • While setting lotions are flexible for all hair types, sculpting lotions are lighter. Both should only be used if it doesn't weigh the hair down.

Maintenance for Chemically Treated Hair

Hair that has been colored or straightened gives you twice the motivation to give your hair the proper moisture. Remember, there is no way to repair damaged hair outside of the use of scissors. Once it's dead, it's dead. Use the following rules (not tips, but *rules!*) for keeping your hair in the best condition possible-and out of the barbershop:

➢ Chemically treated hair should be shampooed at least once a week, followed by deep conditioning.

➢ Heat is no longer your friend so the hooded dryer is the best way to go for drying. Avoid the blow dryer as much as possible.

➢ Minimize the usage of heated styling tools by using the roller set options for curls or wrapping the hair for straight styles.

➢ If you begin having dry scalp issues after the process, go back to my suggestions on oils to soothe the scalp. Sometimes a little witch hazel can cleanse the scalp without vigorous massaging while it also conditions the scalp.

➢ Sleeping with a silk scarf, bonnet or pillow will help eliminate breakage while you're catching some ZZZ's. Cotton pillowcases absorb the needed oils in your hair causing it to frizz.

Maintenance for Natural Textures

Maintaining a healthy head of hair that works with your lifestyle ensures that you're sending out the right message. Wearing your hair in its natural state frees you from a lot of required trips to the salon and has overall lower maintenance, thus less expensive. Take note of some of the following rules of keeping up with your beautiful natural tresses.

➢ Keep in mind that kinky and coily hair, both have raised cuticles so they are naturally become very dry and brittle if not cared for regularly.

➢ Shampooing the scalp and conditioning the hair keeps hair at the right balance of cleanliness and moisturization. If you're not up for constantly washing the hair, simply rinsing with hot water and massaging the scalp is enough to do the trick. (Shampoos haven't been around forever, you know?)

➢ Be sure to get the correct shampoo and conditioner based on your hair type and less based the packaging of the product. Those cool graphics can't save your hair from over drying.

➢ Detangle your hair and let the kinks, coils, curls and waves clump back together while rinsing out just enough conditioner to keep the hair soft, but not overloaded.

➢ Apply product when your hair is still dripping wet and then squeeze the excess water out, allowing the hair to take its natural shape. Do not run your fingers through the hair at this point which will disturb the shape.

➢ Never brush your natural hair when it's dry. Handle all tangles while you're conditioning the hair and do so very carefully, starting from the bottom of the strands and working your way up to the roots.

No matter what hair type you fall under, it deserves the very best treatment just like the rest of your body. Your hair says a lot about who you are so be bold when you showcase it and to be sure that you're confident when doing so, here are my recommendations on each hair type based on the hair shape.

Just because I'm mixed doesn't mean that I'm confused about the uniqueness of my hair. I know that no product can make me exquisite, I just happen to be born this way.

I Know How to Work the "Spot" Light

The toughest thing about being in the "spot" light is the critics. Not only are you self conscience about yourself because you know that you're different, but you're also pretty sensitive to the comments made about you from others. Most times they come from people that you actually like. Other times they come from people that you don't particularly care about, but the moment they attack you with criticism, you're horribly offended.

Girls are the worst critics of them all because most times their comments aren't even about you, they're just towards you. Growing up in my predominately black community at my predominately black school, the girls would search high and low to find something to put me in my place. As odd as I felt, they could have taken a lot more shots than they did, but because I was so likeable as a friend their attempts weren't as bold.

I always knew when someone was warming up to pick a fight with me. It would start off with a side look and grow to the occasional remark about a hair bow popping off or my zipper being down. Something really simple that was just enough to let me know that I wasn't all that. Many of the girls had started out as my friend, but as soon as they saw my mother, I became a target for ridicule. I still get irritated sometimes as an adult when someone makes a fuss over my clothes or my hair because it still feels like I'm being picked on again.

"Svenya, is that a Tommy Hilfiger shirt you're wearing?" one girl asked.

"Uh, I guess." I shrugged as I tried to figure out if that was the name of a pattern or the new word for a button down polo.

I actually had gotten it as a hand me down from a neighbor. By the time I knew what a *Tommy Hilfiger* shirt was, I had outgrown the shirt and had passed it down to someone else-although I doubt that it was ever a *Tommy Hilfiger* brand.

What she was really asking was if I was wearing a knock off *Tommy Hilfiger* shirt and trying to pass it off as a real one. I guess my answer showed her that even if she *did* try to pick on me, I wouldn't get what she was talking about anyway, so she left it alone. That, or she was trying to decide whether or not she should jump me later for it.

My fashion sense and common sense had never been very keen from the start. A time prior to that in the third grade, someone had given me a cool shirt amongst other clothing in a full trash bag of hand me downs. It was red, white and blue with lots of stars all over it. I really liked stars. As I pulled the shirt out of the bag and laid it out to wear the next day at school, my mom said, "No, find another shirt."

So I did. I found another shirt to put *on top* of it until I got to school. The next day on my walk to school, I peeled off my long sleeve shirt like Superman and tossed it into my book bag. As I strolled into my classroom, I saw my two teachers look at each other, but neither of them said a word. By lunch time, I guess it had become too unbearable to watch so one of them must have gotten a shirt out of the lost and found and told me to put it on. Out of obedience I did as I was told after I explained that I had another shirt in my bag and would rather wear it.

Once I got home, the shirt mysteriously disappeared. Many years later as I drove by my dorm in Columbia, South Carolina, I was reminded of that shirt as I looked up at the Confederate flag flying above the State House. I just shook my head. What an idiot I must have looked like! A mixed black girl wearing a Confederate flag shirt strolling around as if it made me a super hero! What was I thinking?

The funny thing about it all is that I don't feel the need to apologize for wearing a neon green Hilfiger knock off or a giant Confederate flag across my chest. While just a little embarrassed, I've learned that that's just the quirky person that I've come to be. In both instances, I was totally naïve to brand names or being politically correct. I was too young to know and too oblivious to care. My idea of owning the "spot" light was all about me being who I was and caring less about the details.

Somehow I lost that idea when going through my teenage years and into my young adult life. Somehow I stopped looking at what was in me and started looking for what was around me that I could emulate. Thank God that only lasted for awhile or I would have been in big trouble because there was nothing around me but chaos!

Working the "spot" light first starts with the light in you. Being comfortable and happy about the decisions that you make starts way before you're able to step out on stage. Don't be afraid to express yourself as long as you do it in a way that that makes you proud of yourself. You're not perfect, you'll make mistakes and you'll definitely make a fool out of yourself every now and then. But life is so short and too imperfect to strive to be anyone else but yourself.

"Is It Because I'm Black?" -Just One of the Sayings that Mixed People Like Me Aren't Allowed to Say…But I Do

Nine out of ten times yes, it's true. It's because I'm black. Or something similar to it. Or let's just say my skin looks like most black people. Or Latina. Or… well, the specifics are a little sketchy, but the bottom line is that I'm definitely not white.

"Is it because I'm black?"

It's funny how that question is taken as a means of confrontation when I ask any non-black person. Those words are as we call them, "fighting words." Ask any white person that question and they discretely look for the nearest point of security. That or they quickly explain to you about how many black friends they have as a way of defusing the issue. Ask that same question to a black person and you get, "Girl, you aren't black." Either way, my question gets dismissed.

I'm not sure where this phrase came from, but something tells me it came from a small child growing up in the sixties who was told by a white person that they couldn't drink from a water fountain or that they couldn't use the so called "public restrooms." Whatever the case, it came from a heart of innocence, of a child hearing the rules of being out in public from his mother before going shopping for school clothes. A mother that said, "Now be sure to use the bathroom before we leave because we're going downtown." Children learn the rules of the game way before it's verbally laid out to them. They just don't know why the rules exist.

There's really no polite way to answer the question and I think that's what makes people nervous. It makes me wonder what a person could say in response to a child asking. How someone with a good conscience could say to a child that yes, their skin color is the reason why they don't have the rights of a human being? I've never heard the question asked without the response being a complete denial of one's race consciousness and a diversion attempt by changing the subject. The attempts can often be comical actually. Some answers go into a full out conversation about a black relative that they have on their cousin's side of the family and how they make the best potato salad - anything to keep the conversation light and non-confrontational.

As creative as those stories get, if I describe the scenario of what just happened to one of my black friends, most times I get some type of snide remark about how I'm not even qualified to ask the question.

"Ahh girl, you're just half black. They could have let you pass." Or "Well Svenya you're not really that black."

Wait a minute. When did I become *half* of a person and what does it mean if I'm not *really* black? Are you only friends with half of me? Do you think I'm passing myself off as black? Why do my black friends think I have it so easy? To me, *those* statements are "fighting words." Twice in the same day has my identity has been dismissed, but they think I have it easy?

When you're mixed, people like to see you as a compilation of things, and to a point this is very true. Parts of our cultures become intertwined with each other so that we don't see things from one angle-and that's a beautiful thing. There are too many variations of religions, customs and languages in the world to not have a broader perspective other than your own.

Unfortunately, there are those that only see the part that's closest to who they are and that's the only part of us that they're willing to accept. I get it. It's fine if all of my interests don't appeal to you, but don't take away my eligibility of being a full person because *you* don't understand the other parts of *me*. I don't know what's worse, a partial friend with set terms of acceptance or a complete stranger denying my value because of my skin color.

Either way, I'm going to make the call that I most certainly *do* qualify to make this statement or any other statement based upon my race because that's what it is, it's MY race. Not theirs.

I get so tired of people saying that mixed people only claim one race when it's convenient for us. When we're looking for financial aid, we're this, when we're trying to get a job promotion, we're that. So what? Everyone else around us gets to determine what they want us to be so why can't we? Should we be qualified for Affirmative Action? Absolutely! We've been denied access to certain rights just as other ethnicities so why wouldn't we?

You have the right to work the "spot" light any way that you please too. It's your right as a person of purpose to determine what you choose to be. You don't have to choose any one exclusively because *you* own *your* "spot" light and *you* call the shots.

Lights, Camera, Action!

Part of being biracial is having attention drawn to you because of your appearance or because your family's color structure doesn't quite look like the typical family. You're not quite white, you're a little black, you're almost Asian or you're not all the way Latina. When people see you, they assume that your lifestyle is a little out of the ordinary and because of that you're often put in what I call the "spot" light. While being in the "spot" light isn't always where we feel comfortable, it's actually a hidden blessing in our DNA that gives us the opportunity to be more than average. At first glance, you've already gained attention and the light is drawn upon you, but instead of shying away from it, let's be sure you give the world a phenomenal performance.

Your performance in life comes from your very own life purpose, which flourishes through all of the little details about you. Every life experience is simply part of the plot and it takes each scene to make the story complete. Nothing that happens in your life is a mistake. Even the bad times have been put there in order to make an amazing ending to the story. Working the "spot" light is about being comfortable in your performance, knowing that the show can't go on without you. You're the star of the show!

But make no mistake about it, being the star of the show is no picnic. There are some things that you'll have to endure that others won't. Aside from the critics and the people watching that wish that it were them on stage, two of the inevitable challenges come from the lighting. The same light that's directed at you so that you have the audience's attention also comes with the discomfort of a glaring beam of light and heat.

Oh yes, the "spot" light isn't for everyone! Only those that can stand the light and take the heat are made for this type of showcase.

Growing up biracial not only means that the "spot" light is shun on you, but that you are automatically given the duty to perform. The light of distraction may come from those that ridicule you or call you names, but it's up to you to keep performing. Keep working towards your dreams knowing that those types of distractions are just part of the "spot" light. Besides, if everyone in the room had a "spot" light shun on them, there wouldn't be any spotlight at all, now would there? Your opportunity to be the star of the show was given to you the day you were born along with the strength and purpose to endure it.

Before I learned how powerful the "spot" light was, I saw it more as a target. The more I stood out, the easier it was for people to pinpoint how different I was so I shun away from the light or got nervous standing in it. I didn't want to be an exception to the rule. Later in life, I learned to appreciate the "spot" light because it gave me power –the power to spice things up and make things more interesting. Who wants to be ordinary anyway?

Through the different scenes of experiences, I became accustomed to the "spot" light and you will too. After awhile, you'll be able to perform in the glaring and distracting light without even breaking a sweat. The distractions will still be there the heat isn't going anywhere, as people will continue to make their own judgments about who you are. But as long as the "spot" light is shining on you, you're still in charge of the performance. Only *you* can determine how it all plays out. Nope, the "spot" light isn't made for amateurs.

Hey Molly, Go Fetch Me Some Water

My last few years of high school were pretty tough for me. It started with my first year when I decided to try out for the Lettergirl Squad. The Lettergirl Squad was the traditional name for the school's dance team. The night before tryouts, my friends and I practiced and practiced until we thought our bones were about to break. From high kicks to the corny dance routine, we were determined to make the team. At the time, only one black girl was able to wear the green and gold uniform, but it was probably because no black girls had really tried out for it. It was only the second year that the school system had begun busing some of us inner-city school kids to my school out in the suburbs. Before then, there wasn't much of an "urban" population as one teacher once pointed out.

Well, long story short, I made the team. So did my friends from middle school Kellie and Jessica. I was so excited to make the team that I could barely see straight. The eczema on the back of my thighs had started to clear up and I was eager to try on my new short skirt. I hadn't worn anything higher than just above my knees in years and I was ready to show off what I was working with.

116

The first day of practice however, didn't go as exciting as I had hoped. All of the white girls barely spoke to us. Not the welcome we were expecting. After a couple of days of the most boring dance practices I had ever experienced, we were called in for a meeting with our parents to discuss the sudden drop out of some of the team members. Apparently, the white girls were upset that we had joined the team and because of reasons that they never really explained, they decided to leave the squad.

"Is it because we're black?" I wanted to ask. But I already knew the answer.

Even though they got quite a shock when my mom entered the room with me, they had made their decision and quite frankly, I could care less. I was hurt because the girls didn't feel like I deserved to be there, but my excitement of being on the team kind of burned away those feelings. By that time, I was quite used to the rejection. Sadly enough, that wasn't the last time someone doubted me based on my brown skin.

My senior year in high school, I was entered into the school's pageant. Prior to that year I had absolutely no idea what that meant, but I was voted by my homeroom to be a contestant so I went for it. I ran a pretty tight schedule between dance classes and working after school so all I needed to know was what time I needed to be there and what I needed to wear. Once that was established, I grabbed a few things at the mall and borrowed a dress from one of my friends who was a frequent pageant star. Once I got to the rehearsal, I realized that I was in something a little more complicated than a fashion show. It involved an interview, standing up straight and a whole lot of smiling. What had I signed up for again?

Most of the girls were well schooled in the pageantry world and they didn't have a problem with announcing it either. The night of the pageant, I rocked my jean dress with a matching hat accented by a flower, and my sparkly borrowed gown for the formalwear competition. Before I knew it, I was crowned Miss Independence High

School Carousel Queen. I still didn't know what being the queen meant except that I would be in the Thanksgiving Parade on a float. It sounded pretty cool to me, although I would have been in the parade anyway as a dancer with the school band. Well, at least now I didn't have to walk.

The following month, I somehow pulled of being crowned homecoming queen too. This competition was different because it was based upon my classmates voting instead of a table full of judges like the pageant. I was in total shock and so was my Dad, who was my escort. That night was a night to remember. It was the first time that I ever had both my parents and Mamma T at my football game to see me dance. I was surrounded by my friends and family and it felt like my wedding day. I felt beautiful and loved.

Not only were my closest loved ones with me, but I had been voted by my classmates as their homecoming queen. Wow, what an honor.

It was rumored that in the school's history, only one other person had won both titles and she definitely wasn't of color. I didn't think much of it when people mentioned it to me. I didn't even know trivial facts like that were even tracked. All I knew was that for the first time, I was accepted for being me. Until the next day.

Just like the girls from the dance team, none the white girls wanted to speak to me that day. The one time I heard a comment, it was more directed *about* me than it was *to* me.

"I just don't think it's fair that someone can win both titles. Give someone else a chance." Kristy said while sitting right behind me.

What did I ever do to her? She wasn't even voted on the court! Besides, where were these opinions when it was time to vote?

That particular morning, the morning announcements on the PA system didn't even recognize me or any of the homecoming events that had just taken place that Friday evening. Not even the final score to the game-which didn't matter because we never won a game anyway.

By then I was pretty ticked off and I became a little more vocal about it. Other racial occurrences happened that year that had disturbed some of my friendships with classmates I had known since middle school, but I didn't care. I was fed up and I did away with the white side of me for the rest of the school year. If they were going to be mad at me for being black, I was going to wear that title and wear it well. After that year, I never had to think about what race to check on a survey ever again.

At the end of my freshman year of college, I joined the University of South Carolina Coquettes- another fancy way of saying the school's dance team. Weekend after weekend for most of my college life, I danced my heart out while on the field in front of over 80,000 people. Some of my closest friends were from my squad and thankfully so, because we spent more time with each other than we did with our roommates. During a few seasons I was the only spot in a leotard, but by then I was enjoying all of the attention. I may have been dancing in front of a couple thousand rednecks wearing Confederate flags on their underwear, but while in the stadium we all bleed garnet red. What I remember most were the bright eyes of the little girls' faces from the stands that couldn't take their eyes off of me. Whether they were brown, blue or green eyes, it didn't matter. I enjoyed for those few minutes of entertainment, being something that they hoped to be.

It's funny how the "spot" light can make or break a person. It can either be too much pressure or just enough pressure to make them stronger. I personally believe that there's never too much pressure. There are just times when a person doesn't have enough faith-faith in who they are. But it's in those times that we're called to dig deeper into ourselves. Everyone has life experiences that pull out some pretty hurtful things, but that's where our strength comes from. If it weren't for those challenges, we'd be skating through life without a mission of purpose, without a reason to help another person, without learning anything about ourselves. That's no way to live. It's not even living. Where's the excitement in that?

Being biracial has shown me that life itself is a beautiful thing. It reminds me every day that the world isn't about me. There are too many unfamiliar things for me to think otherwise. I embrace who I am and I've learned to work the "spot" light because I know that I've been given the chance to be seen in a way that allows me to showcase my uniqueness without ever being bashful or ashamed of being different. I can't expect the audience to appreciate my performance if I can't appreciate the opportunity to perform. It took Molly in my dance class to show me just how different I was and since then, I've learned to keep dancing with my head up and shoulders back. The show has just begun and I've got a whole lot of performance left in me!

Just because I'm mixed, doesn't mean that I have to be confused, ashamed of or undecided about for who I am. God lives in me, as me.

Bill of Rights for Racially Mixed People

Written by Maria P. P. Root (first published in 1996)

I have the right

- not to justify my existence in this world

- not to keep the races separate within me

- not to be responsible for people's discomfort with my physical ambiguity

- not to justify my ethnic legitimacy

- to identify myself differently than strangers expect me to identify

- to identify myself differently than how my parents identify me

- to identify myself differently than my brothers and sisters

- to identify myself differently in different situations

- to create a vocabulary to communicate about being multiracial

- to change my identity over my lifetime--and more than once

- to have loyalties and identify with more than one group of people

- to freely choose whom I befriend and love

Your Personal Journey of Discovery

Every single one of you has inspired me to open up to you about who I've grown to be, something I never did as a child. You've heard me talk about my experiences and I've given you my sincerest advice on living your life with as much purpose as possible and with no regrets. When it comes down to it, we aren't a statistic. Statistics are for those with the exact same makeup. We're too diverse to be considered a statistic. We're individually unique but being judged based upon the opinions of people that inevitably don't even matter! Being mixed but not confused is about taking pride in your unique blend of heritages while also having the power to share it with others.

We often think that what we see on the outside is all that's there, but that couldn't be further from the truth. There's more than meets the eye and fortunately for the outside world, they will be able to see all the many details of you that lie underneath the skin. We're all anxious to hear what you've got to share.

Here's your chance for a little self discovery where you'll get a chance to talk about your experiences and thoughts. As I said in the beginning of our journey, everyone's story is different and we've all been through experiences in life that have made us who we are today. Of all of the people that I've spoken to on being mixed, I've yet to hear the same story twice. I look forward to hearing yours next.

The following questions may bring up things in your past that you didn't realize how much they had affected you. Other questions may bring up a group discussion as there's always more than one way to look at the puzzle. Blogs about some of these issues are posted up on the website for your chance to respond.

Take a little time to answer the questions by writing down your answers. If you'd like to share them, please send them to me. I'd love to hear about your experiences and I'll be using some of your stories for the following books to come. The power of your words is sure to inspire hope for someone else that's looking for the same answers.

If you do decide to share your thoughts, don't forget to give me your name, the background of your heritages, the city and country of where you live and your age. Throw in a picture too, if you'd like, so I can place a name with a face. There's no pressure to use your real name if you don't want to, I just want to hear what you have to say!

Now, let's take a look at you so that I can get to know just how special you are. Congratulations, you're now in the "spot" light!

Share With Us and Join the Revolution

Feedback to the following questions can be sent to:

Svenya@swirlpower.com

www.SwirlPower.com

www.facebook.com/swirlpower

What does being biracial mean to you?

_____
_____
_____
_____
_____
_____
_____
_____
_____
_____
_____
_____
_____
_____
_____
_____
_____
_____
_____
_____
_____
_____
_____
_____
_____
_____
_____
_____
_____
_____
_____
_____
_____
_____
_____

What experiences have you faced that no one seems to understand?

_____
_____
_____
_____
_____
_____
_____
_____
_____
_____
_____
_____
_____
_____
_____
_____
_____
_____
_____
_____
_____
_____
_____
_____
_____
_____
_____
_____
_____
_____
_____
_____
_____

When did you know that there was something different about you?

_____
_____
_____
_____
_____
_____
_____
_____
_____
_____
_____
_____
_____
_____
_____
_____
_____
_____
_____
_____
_____
_____
_____
_____
_____
_____
_____
_____
_____
_____
_____

Family Experiences: What is/was your family life like growing up?

_____

_____

_____

_____

_____

_____

_____

_____

_____

_____

_____

_____

_____

_____

_____

_____

_____

_____

_____

_____

_____

_____

_____

_____

_____

_____

_____

_____

_____

_____

What culture(s) do you relate to the most? Why?

Hair Stories: Tell me about your best hair secrets and worst hair nightmares.

_____
_____
_____
_____
_____
_____
_____
_____
_____
_____
_____
_____
_____
_____
_____
_____
_____
_____
_____
_____
_____
_____
_____
_____
_____
_____
_____
_____

What do you hate most about being biracial or multiracial?

What do you like about being biracial or multiracial?

What principle from this book do you think is the most important lesson? Why?

_____
_____
_____
_____
_____
_____
_____
_____
_____
_____
_____
_____
_____
_____
_____
_____
_____
_____
_____
_____
_____
_____
_____
_____
_____
_____
_____
_____
_____
_____
_____
_____
_____
_____
_____
_____

What types of family traditions do you take part of that most of your friends don't know much about?

_____
_____
_____
_____
_____
_____
_____
_____
_____
_____
_____
_____
_____
_____
_____
_____
_____
_____
_____
_____
_____
_____
_____
_____
_____
_____
_____
_____
_____
_____
_____
_____
_____
_____

What's part of your life's purpose and how do you plan on using it to work the "spot" light?

_____

_____

_____

_____

_____

_____

_____

_____

_____

_____

_____

_____

_____

_____

_____

_____

_____

_____

_____

_____

_____

_____

_____

_____

_____

_____

_____

_____

_____

_____

_____

_____

_____

_____

_____

_____

Freestyle: What else would you like to share?

References

Banks, Tyra with Vanessa Thomas Bush: Tyra's Beauty: Inside and Out. New York, HarperCollins, 1998

Dickey, Anthony. Hair Rules! The Ultimate Hair Care Guide for Women with Kinky, Curly, or Wavy Hair. New York: Villard, 2003

LaFlesh, Teri. Curly Like Me: How to Grow Your Hair Healthy, Long and Strong. Hoboken, New Jersey, 2010

Root, Maria P.P.. Racially Mixed People in America. Newbury Park, California, London, United Kingdom, New Dehli, India: Sage Publications, 1992

Taylor, Susan C., M.D. Brown Skin: Dr. Susan Taylor's Prescription for Flawless Skin, Hair, and Nails. New York: HarperCollins, 2003

Photo Credits

Book cover and back cover shot by Matthew Jordan Smith

Book cover and back cover hair and makeup by Damien Salter

Book cover styling by Jason Griffin

Back Book cover make-up by Terrell Mullin

Book cover by Tony Reese of Reese Design Group

Book photos collected by the author and Matthew Jordan Smith